I0620162

HITTING

An Engineer's
Notes on
Disability

MY STRIDE

R. Shrivaths Iyengar

Copyright © 2023 R. Shrivaths Iyengar

ALL RIGHTS RESERVED
No part of this book may be translated, used, or reproduced in any form or by any means, in whole or in part, electronic or mechanical, including photocopying, recording, taping, or by any information storage or retrieval system without express written permission from the author or the publisher, except for the use in brief quotations within critical articles and reviews.

Limits of Liability and Disclaimer of Warranty:
The authors and/or publisher shall not be liable for your misuse of this material. The contents are strictly for informational and educational purposes only.

Warning—Disclaimer:
The purpose of this book is to educate and entertain. The authors and/or publisher do not guarantee that anyone following these techniques, suggestions, tips, ideas, or strategies will become successful. The author and/or publisher shall have neither liability nor responsibility to anyone with respect to any loss or damage caused, or alleged to be caused, directly or indirectly by the information contained in this book. Further, readers should be aware that Internet websites listed in this work may have changed or disappeared between when this work was written and when it is read.

Cover & interior design: Stefan Merour
Editing: Anaik Alcasas
Author photo: Madhavi Gosalia

Printed and bound in the United States of America

ISBN: 979-8-218-27560-0

माता, पिता, गुरु, दैवम

(The Mother, the Father, the Teacher, the Divine)

"There are more things in heaven and earth,
Horatio, than are dreamt of
in your philosophy."

– William Shakespeare, Hamlet (1.5.167–8)

Contents

ZERO

I was two months shy of my fifth birthday when I ran for the last time.

It was 1988. I'd topped my class and couldn't wait to tell my parents. When I stepped off the school bus in that busy Delhi neighborhood, I could see my mother across the street, and my excitement took over. As I ran over to tell her my grades, I completely missed the distracted driver in his truck speeding straight toward me.

It took the efforts of many surgeons, physical therapists, and prosthetists to get me walking again. To this day, it remains the second most frightening thing I've been through.

The story I'm about to tell you in this book qualifies as the most frightening thing.

That kind of irreversible change could feel deeply troubling; you feel like you've been knocked off whatever path you were headed down. I lucked out because no one told me, aged five, what I could've been had I still been left with two functioning legs. Instead, I simply watched my family and friends, and doctors chart out a new course, and I followed. Whenever I was told, "Nothing has changed, and nothing will change," there was never any reason for me to question it. Life still just worked according to plan, our plan, the one we seemingly always had.

The certainty of knowing a plan existed gave me a measure of comfort at a time when so much felt unknown. This plan consistently emphasized independence to achieve normalcy. Even considering how much of it must have been invented along the way, I trusted our plan despite all its contradictions and contingencies. Really all I needed to do was stay the course. I simply needed to be meticulous, persistent, and stoic. And truthfully, the plan has worked out surprisingly well; after all, I'm still around to talk to you.

Despite our plan guiding me through an education and all the way to employment, it was still drafted in complete chaos. And I'd done everything I was told would be hard, because our plan seemingly broke through every difficulty I'd seen. Each time it worked, I never asked how or why it did. I followed it diligently but unknowingly because it was "our plan" not "my plan." Like a high-school student sitting in a seemingly interminable exam, I knew what worked, not why, and that was no longer good enough. And while a youthful affection allowed me to ignore its warts, I felt I should've gained the experience to craft something better by now.

So when my thirtieth birthday approached, with it came a vague lump of unease. In the following weeks, that lump continued to grow. Every day, for months, I stared blankly through a computer screen, trying to figure out why despite succeeding I still felt like a failure; and over those same months, every night, I crumpled onto my bed, knowing that I wasn't any closer to an answer.

I'd known for a while that although my life was moving faster than ever, it was also more stagnant than it had ever been. I was approaching the age my parents were in '88, and I knew more about my disability than we did then.

Back when I was five years old, I learned how to walk again by setting goals and applying patterns. You walk five feet, and your reward is a target fifteen feet further; you solve that problem by repeating your first walk three more times.

Easy.

But now, when I should be able to think miles ahead by looking just as far back, I found myself unable to move.

When standing on prosthetic legs, few things are more terrifying than a creeping sense of unstable ground. I couldn't picture that next target because now when I looked back, all I could think was, How I did make it this far?

Perhaps I shouldn't have been surprised. It's not easy to find fault with something you've lived day after day for over three decades. But even I can admit that the last few years of executing the plan consisted of frantic rehashes held together with prayer. As the year passed, the feeling of urgency increased, as did the festering worry in my mind that I couldn't invent that next step.

So, I did what I always do when I don't know where to go: I stayed put. I stayed exactly where I was and waited. And tried to figure out my next steps.

I wanted to believe that I wasn't alone or even the first to run into this. There must've been others before me with that growing sense of unease; others who'd had to think about how long their disabilities would allow them to function. They would've thought long and hard about how to survive, and perhaps that would explain my quandaries too. These were such obvious questions, I assured myself, that someone, some-where, would have answers, and I only needed to find them.

That didn't quite work. There are many stories of accomplish-ment and activism, and they are, without a doubt, inspira-tional. But, for someone like me, who's lived and wants to live a regular, unremarkable, normal life, all I found, after many months of searching, were examples of exceptionalism.

The lives of Byron, Beethoven, Kahlo, and Keller are so far removed from mine that they are more overwhelming than educational. As someone with neither their discipline nor their skill, I can no more learn about how to live from Hawking than I can from watching House MD.

I've seen plenty of instances where those with a disability are rightfully venerated. But I needed advice, not inspiration.

There has always been a disconnect between those who endure and those who adore. Somewhat curiously, it was that same disconnect that suggested the beginnings of an answer. As I read those stories myself and listened to others who'd read them, I realized the gap in my reasoning. The lived experience of someone with a disability, that mechanical day-to-day they endure, can't be contained within a single story. Those individual steps, that detail, is only understood with an introspective eye, not an awestruck one. And as my year of confusion made abundantly clear, I don't know how to truly explain my disability or how I've managed to work with it for so long.

Don't get me wrong, I know how to describe it, and I know how to manage it; I can go into detail about how it originated and how it presents itself. I've learned how to phrase it anatomically, surgically, and behaviorally.

But I could only explain it for three decades as what was lost, not what survived. And it's why, when I desperately needed to ask those around me to help me find an answer, I couldn't even begin to frame the question.

If I knew only the barest minimum about where I was and knew even less about how I got there, figuring out where I was headed wouldn't be easy. Granted, I've been told who I was going to be many times. It was quite the mix of expecting me to be an inspirational over-achiever and responding with shock that, "Oh my goodness, you got out of bed on your own!" But those responses were always from those who saw me but didn't truly know me. Which is why the answer couldn't start with them.

Somewhere in my head, ticking away, was everything I'd learned from those who truly knew me—my family, friends, teachers, coworkers, doctors, and even neighbors. Their expectations of me never changed because of my disability because they focused on what I still had.

One of their expectations must have been that when a new plan became necessary, I'd be able to figure one out or know myself well enough to ask for help. I'd look for someone else or something else to give me the push they've been giving me for so long. But that hadn't happened and the uncertainty, the lack of self-awareness, scared me.

The cause of my unease gradually became clearer: the utility of my former plan had run out and I had no idea how to invent a new one.

Zero

This fretting began shortly after my thirtieth birthday and could've continued endlessly, but a few months later, at my friends' insistence, I left my cocoon and joined them for dinner.

That Friday the idle chit-chat over pizza kept me half-absorbed while the rest of my brain occupied itself with its still unsolved problem. One of my friends noticed and asked, "Still with us?"

"Uh huh, I'm still here."

"Really?" my friend responded, "Doesn't quite look like it; looks like you've got something else on your mind."

"And you looked confused at the meeting earlier today too. Like you weren't expecting to be there," chimed in another.

"That wasn't … no, it's just … that wasn't the question I expected …" I replied.

"So … everything's okay?" they asked.

"Sort of. Actually, no, not really. Something's been bugging me for a while, and I haven't been able to figure it out."

"Okay …" one of my friends said. "You want to talk through it? Maybe you can see it better by saying it out loud."

"Maybe," I admitted. "Okay, here's what I've got so far …"

Part 1

"Fortune favors the prepared mind."

— Louis Pasteur

"You don't have to make your nest on the dome of Queen's palace, O Eagle, choose to reside on the peaks of mountains."

— Allama Iqbal

ODDS

Over the years, I've learned to speak and understand three languages and heard many more. There are two kinds of sentences I have heard, in almost all those languages, from people who hear the story of how my two silvery-looking crutches became lifelong friends. We'll get to the other kind later, but the first is, "You are so, so lucky!"

I know what they mean. They recognize that following the events of '88, I'm lucky I survived and that I can walk. The chain of events that led to where I am today, writing these words, was a highly improbable one. However, their "lucky" assessment, while correct, is incomplete. And as an engineer, I can't let that go.

Appa grew up in the 1950s as one of five in Villupuram, near Cuddalore, in Tamil Nadu, a coastal Southern Indian state. He had trained as an engineer and after an undergraduate degree at a university in southern India, he found his first job miles away in the north.

After getting married to Ma and moving house several times, Appa moved with his wife and new young daughter to North India again to continue working for the government in the 1980s. Then, three years into the eighties, I showed up, crying and asking for baby food.

Despite a less-than-ideal start economically, the presence of a language barrier, and a newly independent India still finding her footing, our family settled in the capital city of Delhi. When I was four, Appa learned of new flats (or apartments if you prefer) and decided to buy his own in a newly built block. That became our home starting January 1988 and has been ever since.

His initial moves all over India turned out to be just the start. The Indian government does one thing well for its employees—it offers them its on-the-job training through a lively ride all over the country. Midway through 1988, that same career took him out of his newly-moved-in home to Odisha (then Orissa) in Eastern India. Knowing that this could be the first of many such remote postings we went on with our lives in Delhi and waited for him to finish his tour.

Nine months after we had moved in, a truck decided to vehemently disagree with me on who deserved to stand at a given spot in the road. Appa was several hundred miles away and had to be notified by telegram.

Three months later, I could sit up again.

Despite everything, I was lucky. The Indian government could've sent Appa anywhere, but he ended up in Delhi. Within a decade of moving to a relatively unfamiliar city, he had bought a house, even though at that stage of his career, it was rare to have extended employment in any city.

Delhi had, at the time, some of the premier hospitals with the best-known doctors in the country, and one of those hospitals was not too far from where we lived. At that hospital, after my accident and while Appa traveled back to Delhi, the doctors who worked on me likely saw a problem with no simple answers and lots of difficult choices. And yet, every single one of their bets has paid off to this day.

We'll get to that eventually. Before that, I need to tell you about Ma.

Ma was the eldest sibling of three, and the only daughter. Most of the stories she told me about her childhood were about time spent in Ooty and Chennai in Tamil Nadu, a coastal state in Southern India. Her father, my grandfather, was one of the old-school disciplinarian sorts, but in Ma's telling, he doted on his independent daughter.

Once Ma got married to Appa, figuring out how to keep a family comfortable when frequently moving house may well have prepared her for constantly balancing multiple variables. Ma's exacting standards, like her father's, also required my older sister Dee and me to ace every class we attended, irrespective of circumstances.

Of all of Ma's stories, there is one that makes her speak in an uncharacteristically quiet voice. It was in the summer of 1988 and Ma was out shopping with Dee and me at a marketplace when we missed the last bus. We'd had to walk a long while before finding some public transport to take us home. "You were four," she says, "I still think about how much you walked that day …"

A few days later, I'd learn that I had topped my class for the first time and wanted to run over to tell her. She was standing on the other side of the road when it happened.

The first set of prosthetics took a while to get right, and the group of about four technicians responsible for designing them whooped and clapped loudly when I first walked with them. As handshakes and congratulations were exchanged, I was too young to know that those steps were meant to be challenging, but the smiles of satisfaction on my parents' faces suggested that I'd done something good. It also meant that school was a possibility, eventually, if I could walk on my own. With some shoulder crutches and a basic set of prosthetics, Ma helped me ignore the searing pain in my upper arms and taught me how to walk for the second time in four years. I fell half the time the first few days or weeks, but she was prepared to help me come out on top in this class as well.

In India in the late 1980s and early 1990s, the number of such rehabilitation and prosthetics centers around the country must have been small; to have one in your city at all is rare, and to have one twenty minutes away can only be described as fate.

Being a part of the burgeoning middle class made it possible for us to consider the possibility of prosthetics and rejoining school. But most of all, having family and medical professionals around you who were willing to continue solving infeasible problems was staggeringly lucky, particularly considering how much easier the alternatives may have been.

So, yes, a considerable part of my life has involved chance, and the way it has worked out has seemed to me, at times, to be due to almost criminally good fortune.

But then, I remember Ma stitching cushions to keep me seated upright after I returned home after the surgery. And I remember the wheelchair they carried up step by step, huffing and puffing, to our second-floor home. And years later, Appa, in a moment of rare candor, shared how often he worried in those days about where the money would come from for the inevitable prosthetics when the budget was already maxed out on home maintenance, loans, education, and on and on.

Maybe that's where the truth lies—the work, sweat, blood, tears, and worry our family knowingly spent years ago looks like luck today to those on the outside looking in. Observing things that way is also tempting simply because other explanations are so improbable. It's easier to explain that Appa was destined to get the job he did, Ma was blessed with a strong will, our house brought us fortune, and I'm lucky to be alive; other explanations, burdened with facts, are too hard to believe.

But more importantly, if this indeed was grueling work (as it was), then the only lesson we have isn't in generalizations about luck. It's that, going forward, nothing can ever be left to chance. Every school exam, every lecture in university, every night out with friends, every trip, every job, every illness, every house, every walk, every step, every muscle moved needs forethought. Trips to the beach are for feet that can grip the sand. Dancing in the rain is for those who can afford to slip on damp leaves on the street and get back up. Some of us must have backups for our backups, and for us, spontaneity has a cost. Sometimes that cost is worth the reward, and when it isn't, politely declining isn't hurtful or thoughtful. It's all there is.

Obviously, this calculus constantly racing through my mind has downsides, and those around me would probably prefer if I didn't think, re-think, or even overthink something as simple as a dinner date. But there is also a curious advantage in seeing past a choice to its variables and their outcomes: it makes you unusually aware of chance simply because of the possibilities you can imagine.

Odds

Those who see me imagine a boy growing up with a disability during the '90s in India. Those who know me as you now do, perhaps imagine a boy growing up with a disability in a middle-class home, as the India he lives in enters an era of greater prosperity for more of her people. And despite top notch medical care, this boy could easily have been another disabled statistic if not for the relentless drive and quiet determination of his parents.

You're damned right I'm lucky.

LIAR

"**D**on't look now, by the way, but that kid behind you is loving this story."

Idle comments like that constantly fly among friends over dinner at restaurants. In hindsight, I wasn't telling a particularly remarkable story, just something that happened at work that I thought my friends would find funny.

Most stories demand gravity or excellence or, at the very least, clarity, none of which I can claim to have. I'd never be able to write a memoir, for instance; even the first words would be an overreach, and I would never get to the end. Something that substantial needs far more than a voice; it must be one hell of a story.

So, when I share my notes with you, they must take the form of an explanation. Stories about disability are supposed to be exceptional, and mine are so much more mundane. What you want to hear is about people overcoming hideously tricky conditions, not why I think "bilateral" is a fantastic word.

Seriously, how cool is it that a word meaning two-sided can be used by biology teachers talking about symmetry and newspaper editors writing about international treaties? How could you not marvel at a word so versatile that it spans science and foreign policy!

It's a word of such utility that I must tell you my first memory of encountering that word. I promise I'll be quick because you'd think that it was in school, but it's really from a time when the very idea of my attending school was itself in question.

While researching our options back in '88, we heard of the Jaipur leg, which was nationally known for being a low-cost, indigenously developed prosthetic. Even the little nuggets we knew seemed promising, and we planned a visit interstate to learn more.

Ma and Appa walked around the production facility absorbed in earnest conversation with other grown-ups while I made friends with another kid, not that much older than I was, who'd also lost a leg.

We weren't there for very long, but I have three specific memories: one, the food was too greasy; two, that other kid left with a set of prosthetics well before I did; and three, I remember that he got to ride an elephant before his stay ended.

A few days later, we made our way back to Delhi without the satisfying results we had hoped for. The explanation included phrases like "bilateral above-the-knee cases aren't easy."

I was disappointed and felt mildly jealous of that other kid because of his elephant ride, but also fascinated by the word "bilateral" and perhaps also slightly pleased at being a more complex engineering problem for the super-smart people we'd met.

On our return one thing became clear: this search for someone to design these prosthetics for me was necessary, so even if it took time and energy, that necessity made the search worthwhile.

Getting that first set of legs was just the beginning. And then the second, the third, and the fourth over the following decades. With each set, my family researched more and weighed the pros and cons of British, German, and Taiwanese prosthetic limb manufacturers.

Meanwhile I awkwardly negotiated my way through studies in primary and high school. In those days, while Appa took the bus to work, I went in the family car to high school unaware of his worries and carrying my own. Specifically, just the one about whether this girl I liked also liked me back. She was so intelligent, so literate, and yet so grounded that she even made someone like me believe I could hold a conversation. Or at least try. Once.

"We've been walking for a while now. Are you sure you don't want to stop and rest?" she asked.

"No, no, I'm fine. I just need to balance my weight better on my legs," I lied, hoping my brain would focus on the blood pounding in my heart instead of the lack of feeling left in my leg.

"You know, I've often thought about that."

"What?"

"All the exertion must feel excruciating for your bones. Can you really rest your legs?"

"Sure, I just take them off," I coughed out, doing mental cartwheels over the fact that she chose the word "excruciating" over any more straightforward word available.

"You can take them off?! I thought they were attached to your legs somehow!"

"Wait, you thought my artificial legs were built around and over my real ones?!"

"No, of course not! Don't be silly! But I did think there was some joint where things … attached … permanently."

"What, like Robocop?"

"Who?"

I decided then and there that just as the intricacies of human anatomy and biomechanical hardware weren't common knowledge, so familiarity with an 80s cult classic, despite its clever social commentary, wasn't a prerequisite for conversation.

As we walked back, my palms were sore from gripping my crutches, and my leg had all but abdicated its responsibility towards motor function. But one look at the intelligence and compassion creasing that face as she expressed concern for a teenage boy, and nothing else mattered.

Well into the next day, during my weekend music lessons, I was still floating somewhere in the clouds.

Sorry, we jumped a few steps there; let me explain.

Children of Type-A South Indian families must have at least one other skill besides academics. Thankfully, Dee had picked up classical dance and singing, so I didn't have to (not that I could've, anyway). A process of elimination had led us to the guitar, and as unpleasant as the first few guitar lessons were, I kept going. Not because I appreciated things like discipline and passion and not because I thought I'd be better at other instruments. No, I plowed through those first lessons because when your parents pay with the money they really need elsewhere, when the instructor comes to your house after hours (which he didn't for other kids), and when an entire residential building endures hours of cacophony, you can't reasonably claim to be the only one that's suffering anything.

It took many, many years, but once I broke through that initial stage of tedium and pain, I found myself actually enjoying, even waiting for, that hour on Sunday.

As we make our way from this tangent back to the clouds, you, like me, must surely appreciate the added benefit those lessons offered. Maybe, you see, as I did, that even if I couldn't keep pace with the other boys vying for this girl's attention, my calloused fingers might prove more useful at serenades than gripping crutches.

Teenage crushes aside, the reality was that my current set of prostheses wasn't aging gracefully, and it was time to start on a new set. I wouldn't stand a chance at going on long walks with her if I didn't upgrade to a more comfortable set.

There are few things more draining for me than the process of getting fitted for prosthetics. Some of it is due to physical exertion—like the early stages when casts are being made and require completely shifting my weight off my legs to my shoulders. But the iterative process, spread over different sessions, is just as mentally tiring when we walk the tightrope of choosing between stability and comfort over and over again. And yet, we do it and have done it so many times, knowing that this work, exhausting as it may be, will get us to a better set of prosthetics.

So, when my prosthetist in Delhi saw me grimacing a little during a test stride and asked me where it hurt, I replied, "I'm fine; I probably planted that leg wrong." A few minutes later, it happened again, and I told him, "It's fine, I'm fine; it's probably the alignment."

In a perverse irony, I'd forgotten what I was there for and kept walking till he'd had enough and said, "Something isn't right, stop for a second, and when you know what isn't working, tell me." I gradually slowed down to stop and stared briefly at my teenage reflection in a mirror placed nearby. I saw the sweat dripping from my forehead and felt the pain piercing my right arm and shoulder. I knew exactly what was wrong.

Since my childhood, I've accepted certain things about myself and assumed others would as well. You see, no one can really tell you what a life with a disability will be like because they simply don't know. It's why a description like "It'll be okay" is just as wrong as "It'll be hard," and, practically, all you have to go on is what you know about yourself.

This cliché about disability is why, for the longest time, I was convinced that nothing had actually changed about my life. The pessimists predicted agony, the pragmatists called it effort, and the optimists promised challenges, but everybody all but guaranteed that I'd deal with pain—lots of it, far more than I could handle.

Over the next few decades, as I pretended to roll with the challenges I also became really good at hiding my true state. It's why, when I turned thirty, I could see myself in every mirror and know how scared I felt when I experienced truly unmanageable pain.

And no one ever knew because my disability had made me an exceptional liar.

If pain is the perceived currency of my disability, lies are its transactions.

The optimists believed I was brave and unscathed; to them, I was never whiny or selfish, and my claims of blind luck were self-deprecation.

The pessimists imagined a difficult childhood and a lonely adulthood, and to them, I could not bear rivalries or risk, and my desire for adventure was a pretense.

The pragmatists assumed I was always discovering new nadirs of agony. But to all those who needed me to bear through, I was the picture of stoic certainty.

No matter the reason, no matter the person, I was, and would remain, for all of them, a disabled impostor in an able-bodied world. But two words, "I'm fine," and I get to do what everyone else does. Of course I lied to everyone; it was easy because it was expected.

Remember that girl I fell for in high school and the walk that went nowhere? I told you what I saw in her face, but I didn't tell you much else. What I didn't say was that all she saw in mine was strain, not affection. And if that was how she always saw me, I assumed she would never actually see me or even want to see me. This girl, who I desperately wanted to love, saw nothing but pain in me and got nothing but lies from me.

When I was five, I lost my legs under a truck whose driver barely saw me. And yet, that truth has been far less important than all the lies that followed.

Since then, I've said what I needed to say to secure an education in a world where most disabled kids aren't even sent to school. I've curated a persona in order to be employed in a world where most disabled applicants don't even get to send in their résumés. And in my dating life, you can be sure I'll say what I need to say to avoid pity in a world where most beaches don't lend themselves to long, handicap-accessible walks and where my date might need to hold my crutches more often than my hand.

There are many people like me—unreasonably many—that don't enjoy the prospects and progress I've had, and over all these intervening years, I've been trying to figure out why.

Yet I remember that over those same years, I didn't think that saying "I'm fine" was a lie; it was the barest minimum I could offer, the only way I could get through.

I remember those who wanted nothing less from me than excellence and nothing more for me than peace. The ones who would wince in sympathy when I felt pain and knew all my weaknesses and strengths. The ones that drafted my first plan for me. The ones—like that prosthetist when I was a teen-ager—for whom my lies wouldn't work.

Maybe Appa is right that the long way around isn't as bad, pro-vided the conversation is useful and you still get where you need to be. Maybe Dee and her husband Jeej are right to demand a worthy player for the game. And maybe Ma is right when she suggests that distraction can sometimes help, that assuming my disability is about me is vanity, and that sometimes the right answer to a question is another question.

The builders of my plan deserved an ending far better than what I was giving them.

I may never know how good I can be, but twelve months in 2014 showed me how bad I can get. Yes, "I'm fine" is sometimes my lie, but it hurts less than when you say, "It's okay; I know it's not easy." There are far too many people who put far too much effort into making sure my life could become easy, and they did it by demanding more of me, not less. I know that sometimes that means you'll need to hold my crutches as we take the stairs down, and I'm okay with that; sometimes I want to hold the door open for you, and you need to be okay with that too.

When I tell you that expecting inspiration from me may lead to disappointment for you but expecting nothing of me will feel far worse, will you believe me?

RIVALS

I was right and he was wrong, plain and simple. We didn't need to discuss this any further. But Someone seemed convinced that his approach was the only geometry permitted, and I can be easily bullied into hearing people out, so I gave him the barest courtesy of acknowledging what he said. And when he was done outlining his solution on my Class 5 exam notebook, it made a lot of sense.

But so did mine.

In fact, my solution held up without a single flaw for almost thirty more seconds as he dismantled it line by line, relishing every character he scribbled out.

I certainly didn't deserve the guffaws that followed from the crowd surrounding us. But perhaps, he didn't deserve the pencil thrown at his eye either.

As I insincerely apologized, and he scowled and rubbed the wrong eye, an amused classmate offered this helpful commentary to other hangers-on, "It's an ego clash, but they'll get over it." I haven't, and I won't, and it's because he was right, and I was wrong, and worst of all, he knows it.

Our high school always emphasized this odd mix of competition and cooperation that I never understood back then. At the end of the school year, Someone was expected to top the class, but during that same year, the people most likely to get to the top would've collaborated on some project or another. It drove me up the wall! I wasn't as naturally brilliant as some of these guys, but I was still expected to compete with them. So why in the world was I helping them?

It gets worse! I saw these people day in and day out, and they were nice to me! When something didn't quite make sense in class, we could count on each other to commiserate over how pointless it all was. When we'd get into trouble together, one would lean on the other to bail us out. One classmate would be ruthlessly creative with a physics problem we were all trying to solve, but when I needed to prep for a competition I could always rely on him to critique my efforts.

I know what you're thinking: if I valued their friendship as much, why wouldn't I move to something else? I tried, I really did, and it didn't work. They found me each time, this army of Someones. I switched from trying to be good at physics to mathematics, and Someone killed me. English went fine till Someone beat me three times in a row, and I switched. At one point, I almost convinced myself that I was bilingual in Sanskrit till Someone aced an exam, while I huffed in jealous exasperation four points behind her.

I could rant for days about how Someone made everything I knew about computers antiquated two days after he joined our school. Or how Someone dominated me in chemistry without even caring that they did. I could go on and on about how every single one of my classmates (these friends!) disarmingly complimented me when I did well, only to thrash me at the next available exam.

The only thing good about any of it was that it prepared me for university. But our university was equally confounding; students slaved for years to get in, and before they could revel in their success that they'd been accepted and arrived, their confidence would get uniformly leveled to "Oh God! Again?!" year after year.

Nothing is more unnerving than being part of an entire class of the most self-assured and ambitious students in India sitting quietly in a massive hall and warily eyeing each other as competition. Four weeks in, the competition for first place was over, but the game continued for second place, and third, and fourth, and so on. I chased and was chased by so many more Someones for four years. And four years later, when members of that same class looked at each other again in the same hall, this time it was with smiles of relief that we'd survived.

Rivalry, for me, is not mania; it's fuel, it's inspiration. Every step could make me feel like an impostor, but the truth is, I wasn't expected to fulfill much of anything anyway. There may be those who think people with a disability would flinch in the face of competition. But the great genius of the game of ambition lies in how all-consuming it is; when it makes you forget food and health, it also makes you forget pain and doubt. Once the game begins, nothing else matters but the players and the game.

I'm not telling you this to inform your suspicions that I'm insanely competitive; you already knew that. If anything, this mania continued well into grad school and work because neither age nor experience matters when you're in this game.

Nor is this an apology to those classmates from school or university for possible friendships ruined in the game. Despite my own personal ruthlessness, university friendships survived. Whether close or only cordial, we retain an ability to pick up our conversation years later exactly where we'd left off.

No, I'm telling you this because the game mattered. It was played with exactly the stakes and at exactly the time it should've been. There are historical duels over skill or romantic conquest, there are rivalries over philosophy or corporate ambition, there are wars for territory, and every one of those is a zero-sum game.

The game I was a part of never had losers for the simple reason that my rivalries were not for the purpose of defeating opponents but rather earning their approval.

And no game has gone on longer than the one I've played with Dee.

She's eight years older than I am, and if you think that doesn't make a difference, tell that to High School Me, who endured six years as his sister's brother. I never mentioned the Someone who could've beaten me at biology when I was in school because that Someone had done it already, eight years prior. I'd envy her the head start she had over me, but for someone smarter and more deliberate than me, that head start was irrelevant.

Worst of all, she's more patient than I am. When Ma was away for two months in the middle of high school, she ran the house, and rather than help, I chose to fall ill. For two months, she studied medicine, attended classes, went to the hospital, and kept us humming. It wasn't till Ma returned and she could goof around again that I realized how much she missed being the kid I could be all the time. Chance had conspired to get me what I wanted, but she had to push to get what she has relentlessly.

Despite all her superiority, I believed I could win; all I had to do was wait it out till she got married. Once that happened, she'd have a family of her own, and I'd be unchallenged in ours.

Part 1

My long con nearly worked except for one minor wrinkle: my brother-in-law Jeej. Where Dee could beat me at finding solutions, Jeej can beat me at decisively implementing them. Whenever Dee could pierce my ego with questions, Jeej now pierces it with better answers than mine.

I had been eagerly preparing for dominance after six years as second fiddle, but with the arrival of Jeej, I now resigned myself to eight more years away from pole position.

Having heard that jeremiad, it's easy to dismiss this absurdly competitive streak as a chip on my shoulder. But consider, if all I wanted were to win, I'd sink to my basest levels (and you know they exist); if all I wanted was to show I'm better, I'd break what they had. While that's certainly an option, it's not one that interests me. Everybody knows that one person whose ruthless competitiveness has set them up for a lonely life, but the great ones tell us that—achievements aside—they're better for having other people in their lives.

I've often noticed how mismatched my rivalry was, but the game still made that mismatch worthwhile. Yes, my climb continues always to get steeper, but I'm not headed up the mountain alone. And yes, I've fallen and bruised myself many, many times, but whenever I fell, that same army of Someones also helped me stand up again.

For many years, I used to walk by steadying my hand on Someone's shoulder. Just as my walk was made better by having their shoulder, my life has been made better by our game.

There are times when I want to be protected, but equally, there are times when that protection feels like an unnecessary crutch. There are times when I don't want to walk, and instead, I desperately want to jump, despite knowing that I'll fall. At those times, I lean on those players who, like my family, know that giving me yet another crutch is unnecessary when I already have two.

We deny ambition to those with disabilities out of a well-intentioned but misplaced desire to protect them. What if they become unhappy at how uneven the playing field is or how many advantages their competition has?

What if they get exhausted by their mountain climb because it's so much steeper for them than everyone else?

And what if when they reached for the stars, they tripped and fell and got hurt?

And truly, what if they did?

The joy of the game is not in knowing that you've won or lost; the joy is in the game itself.

The joy is in knowing that you belong; it is in wanting to do better, to be better.

The joy is in being worthy of the competition; it's in being a worthy competitor for others.

There is also joy in knowing that your being in the game matters, and no one should be denied that joy.

The game matters, as do its players because, rather than crutches, they always give me a target instead.

ABLE

I was in my third year at university and desperately trying to figure out what I would do when I graduated. I didn't get to decide about kindergarten, any of the schools I went to as a child or even university. Hell, I hadn't even had to think about which discipline I would choose in university; when you've only got the one thing that you're slightly good at, the choice isn't a problem. But as I came closer to graduating, the noise in my head grew louder and started thumping: Work or study? Work or study?

Let me roll back the clock to when the thumping noise in my head began in earnest. It was 1996. I was thirteen years old and lounging about in my room, humming a song to myself, and avoiding homework yet again.

Part 1

In hindsight, my room was the worst place to be lounging for a bunch of reasons. The TV sat in the living room, surrounded by all the good books we had in our house. Even our pre-Internet home computer was out of reach in Ma and Appa's room till I was done with homework.

Worst of all, my room wasn't mine alone, it was also my then twenty-one-year-old sister's. Dee had apparently decided to complete all her undergrad years of studying medicine in one uninterrupted, sleep-deprived stretch.

A mind in that state does not look kindly upon the relaxation of younger siblings, which is probably why she broke into my humming by asking what I thought I'd be doing when I was her age. Now, she often used to drift into one of her half-drowsy "ask questions rhetorically" phases. Usually, when Dee asks me what I am planning to do, it's more an opportunity for her to answer her own question with, "Shut up, listen, this is what you're supposed to do."

Assuming this was one of those instances, I pretended to look thoughtful and contemplative. I was only half-right— even though she was wide awake, the question was still rhetorical. She opened her answer again with, "Shut up, listen, this is what you're supposed to do." Then she rattled off the words, "School. Bachelor's. Masters. Work." in rapid succession and went back to her textbooks, leaving bullet holes in my reverie.

You're probably wondering now whether I actually heeded her advice and even if I did, why that's relevant to a thumping noise in my head. A quick recap will help.

The first school I joined with my first proper pair of prosthetics was the same one I attended before I needed any prosthetics at all. That decision made a lot of sense to me with the continuity it offered (yes, obviously, as a six-year-old, I had no real say here, but I liked to pretend I did in a bratty, senatorial way). But in another way, it made a lot more sense both because it was with friends I knew and at a place that was a short, five-kilometer (three mile) commute away.

The next school I joined with my second proper pair of prosthetics was the same one that Dee had attended for five years. This one was also local to where we lived, and the anticipation of proving myself at a new school gave way to the irritation of trying to match up to the genetic expectations Dee—quite the star pupil—had set. But while I grumbled that I'd always be my sister's brother, I'm sure my parents felt relief that I was with teachers who would push me hard while keeping me safe.

And then I prepared to attend university with my third proper pair of prosthetics. (By the way, do you see the connection here? Good for you, because I didn't—not till years later.)

The only two requirements I had of my college experience were that it needed to have the computers I'd come to love, and it needed to let me talk to them. It would be an added bonus if there were also people who weren't put off by my social awkwardness.

But the one requirement my parents had (and which I hadn't considered) was that it needed to be in Delhi.

While we knew of what options were available, we hadn't yet worked through the commute back and forth. We hadn't yet worked out getting around within the university campus; we didn't even know much about the campus; in fact, I didn't know if there was a university that would take me. But while my requirements were expectations, their requirements were actually constraints because we, as a family, hadn't worked out all the variables we needed to.

A surplus of constraints is useful for the same reason that a surplus of choices is not. Having too many choices means you have to pick one at the cost of another; having many constraints means you get to drop possible solutions as you balance one constraint with the help of another.

A university offering a degree in computer science, just like a university in Delhi, could be one of many. But a university in Delhi that offered a degree in computer science and was near our home practically chose itself for me.

That made the next four years surprisingly simple, barring a class schedule that needed a faster, longer walk than I was used to. It's amazing how much the threat of a missed, potentially career-deciding lecture can quicken the pace, even when coordinated across two pairs of fake legs. Ambling wasn't an option, but with friends keeping you company, the to-ing and fro-ing between lecture halls became comfortable. So comfortable, in fact, that two years passed without incident and in relative mental clarity.

Then Year Three started. And with it that thumping noise in my head.

I thought back to Dee's words when I was younger—the "School. Bachelor's. Masters. Work." plan. It seemed like solid advice, and should've made the thumping in my head go silent; after all, if I knew I was going to join a graduate program after university, things should have been sorted, right?

Not quite. Not even close.

Halfway through the four-year undergrad program, most of my classmates had decided on what they wanted to do, and I felt like I'd only just become aware of my choices. For example, I learned that research in the pragmatic computer science field was an option. I realized that I might still manage to make my unrequited love of mathematics amount to something.

But I still felt uncertainty, and with every passing day the thumping grew more intense because I would have to decide on an internship based on the future career that I hadn't yet chosen.

Part 1

Eventually, I decided on a rather magnificent cop-out that came to be known as the Magnificent Plan of Decision Avoidance.

My plan was to do an internship at a research lab abroad, pursue a Master's, and if the two conspired in some way to make me love research, I would then chase a Ph.D.

I was rather proud of my clear-eyed decision-making and was, therefore, confused when my parents responded with an ominous "Think it over a little bit more."

There wasn't anything left to think about, surely—I'd thought about the remainder of my four years (the undergrad), the next six years (the undergrad plus the master's), the next eight years (at which point, either I'm employed or I'm doing something vaguely research-y) and probably even ten years (if I could think that far ahead).

But the conversation following the grand announcement suggested something missing in the plan. I gave up trying to figure it out myself and asked, "What am I missing?"

And then came a barrage of questions that added a whole new level of noise to the thumping in my head.

"Where would you be living in this plan?"

"Will it be easy to get in and out of?"

"If it's not on the ground floor, will you be able to manage?"

"The current set of prosthetics we have is already about four years old, and it won't last more than another three to four years. Ten years down the line, what do you do to replace them?"

"How do you get to and from work?"

"Do you drive? A standard issue vehicle won't work, so what do you drive?"

And on and on it could've gone, except my parents took it easy on me.

It was clear that my Magnificent Plan of Decision Avoidance could not be executed in Delhi itself: it needed an internship at a research lab furthered or substituted by a Master's ... somewhere else ... not Delhi.

If the decision to just find an undergrad university needed the reconciling of so many constraints, there couldn't be a simple way out for anything beyond that.

Choosing something in Delhi meant the ready aid of my parents, the immediate availability of any number of known facilities for emergency prosthetics repair, and many, many doctors who knew the idiosyncrasies of my health.

All these conveniences would disappear if I chose a location outside Delhi; I'd be starting from scratch with no experience in how to move forward.

Thump, thump.

This was possibly the first time it dawned on me that these millions of questions used to spin around in my parents' heads constantly and that surviving '88 was merely the first leg (pun intended) of an exceptionally long marathon.

Whenever a child thinks they've solved everything, their parents' world opens up just a little bit more as if to remind them of all that is still unsolved. The only thing harder than failing to anticipate those questions was the realization that my parents had been preparing me for the marathon the whole time, and I hadn't even noticed.

It's easy to mouth off as a child to amused adults about how you would get a pair of degrees (or more!) intern in Europe, work in the US, and find an appropriately theatrical way to drive off into the sunset. From an eleven-year-old, this speech is considered adorable; unnervingly, a decade later, this is naked ambition verging on fantasy. And those same adults who "aww"-ed at you before are now wondering out loud if those dreams aren't just a teensy bit unrealistic and more appropriate to childhood.

Where a reasonable individual might see logical advice, I could only see affronts. I'd grown so accustomed to seeing the destination and letting everyone else figure out the route that my brain didn't perceive this well-intentioned conservatism as a measured argument; if anything, it saw a glowing match placed tentatively on top of stacks of dynamite and wanted to light it all up.

But a twenty-year-old, planning as haphazardly as I did, still needed a parentally acknowledged "Maybe." ("Yes" isn't ever a possibility because if you work with as many variables as we do, you learn to trust Murphy's Law more than gravity.) I might be able to convince Ma that I would be fine on my own by stressing that I wouldn't really be on my own. Convincing Appa with a logical argument was pointless. There's a reason I have never beaten him at chess. Neither would emotional arguments suffice because even if I was good at those (I'm not) I know they can be deflated with a simple, strategically placed "think logically" in a conversation.

That leaves the third possible line of appeal: other people speaking on my behalf.

Appa had long hoped I might adopt a path not unlike that of the son of one of his close friends. This straight-A man had studied, and then taught computer science at the university I now attended. He had also delivered an impromptu colloquium on the merits of a career in research and academia, and this was one of the first things to clear the confusion in my head about career choices.

In my mind, the fact that this professor (and others) I respected had interned outside India settled things. (That no one thought I could only strengthened my resolve.) So, it was only fitting that a chance remark from him was needed to sway Appa as well.

"He seems to be convinced that he has to study or intern outside India," Appa said as he pointed at me in exasperation. "You've traveled to research labs outside the country. Tell him how difficult it can be."

"Well, do you think you can do it?" he turned around and asked me.

"I have no idea. Depends on what it is, I suppose," I responded uneasily.

"Do you think then that you can manage three months away from family by yourself?"

I replied with the best "Damned if I know" shrug I could muster. His family looked quietly entertained at the matching grimaces on the faces of my family.

"Makes sense," he smiled.

"It does?" the room seemed to ask on my behalf.

"You don't want to say you can't do it because you don't yet know that you can't do it. That makes it worth trying; at least then, you'll have an answer."

A few months after that conversation, I was an intern and waiting for a bus on the streets of Paris.

A year later, I was pacing through grad school in Providence.

A year after that, I was working in Redmond.

The noise in my head hasn't gone entirely, but the question it implies changes every time, as does the reminder that maybe this next gamble will be the one that finally, and quite literally, breaks me.

And yet, in a world that constantly wants to tell me what I can't do, there's something infinitely tempting about wanting to do it anyway.

Ask yourself this: if I walked you over to a massive fireworks display and handed you a match, wouldn't you want to light it up?

Part 2

"There is an art to flying, or rather a knack. The knack lies in learning how to throw yourself at the ground and miss. ... Clearly, it is this second part, the missing, that presents the difficulties."

– Douglas Adams, *The Hitchhiker's Guide to the Galaxy*

"People who know me see me as an ass, treat me as an ass. People who don't know me see a cripple, treat me like a cripple. What sort of selfish jerk wouldn't take advantage of that fact?"

— Dr. Gregory House, MD (played by Hugh Laurie in the television show *House*)

BLAME

Earlier I reflected on the two kinds of remarks I usually get from people who ask what happened to my legs. There was a time when I thought that the commentary from others reflected how their lives were going. So, when someone told me how lucky I was, I could appreciate their infectious optimism. They're the kind of people who endure hours of rain, but it only takes five minutes of sunlight to make them remark, "How gorgeous is the weather we're having!"

I need those happy souls every so often because the more frequent reaction I get is, "It is so sad for this to have happened; why would God do this?"

When I was very young, I only overheard that question and I wasn't sure what a good response would be. I soon discovered that most people decide to make their question rhetorical to spare me the agony of answering.

My family has had a lot of practice enduring such questions.

When I was a bit older, I heard the question directly and responded with various reactions: with improvised innocence, studied innocence, practiced innocence, exasperated innocence, and, finally, bored innocence. I miss those days dearly because I didn't tick off the well-meaning folk as easily then, and whenever I do tick them off these days, I get a mental or physical rap on the knuckles.

The next phase of my growth coincided with a newly-developed sarcastic edge that had me replying to "Why would God …?" comments with snarky comebacks like, "You know, I haven't asked." The problem this posed, however, is that it often led to conflict and discomfort. My Pleased-Bordering-On-Smug Face was usually in stark contrast to my family's Angry Face and the Pained Face writ large on the questioner, accompanied by Nervous Laughter. After the first or second attempt, I dropped this strategy as unworkable.

I later discovered that a far superior alternative is the thoughtful "Hmmm," which serves two purposes: it avoids the question as well as a need to develop an answer, and it gives the questioner the impression that I am considering the pained rhetoric that has creased their face in the moment.

If that sounds about nineteen different kinds of mean and hurtful, it may or may not comfort you to know that I know that it's mean and hurtful. There might be something perverse in me that even enjoys it. The only thing that's changed across all those phases is that I've worked my way from ignorance, to caring, to annoyance, and finally to indifference.

I also fully realize that the pain in the question is real, and my response, unkind as it may be, is no more personal than the abstractness of the question itself. In fact, what grates on me is that the question rests on an assumption that I've trained myself to see as utterly flawed.

You see, I remember very little of the events leading up to that day in '88, and even my memory of what happened on that day is largely second-hand. Why I can't remember is unimportant to me, but across all the variations I heard from those who were there, one thing is crystal clear: I was hit after I ran across the road. Everyone else might have a different recollection they focus on, but that's the most significant one for me. It matters to me that even when I was young, excited, and oblivious to the fact that I was running on a city street, I had control over what I was doing.

Now, look again at that question we started talking about. Do you see the flawed assumption? No, I am not pining for some independence I lost; no, I don't worry about being a burden on others; and yes, you have been watching a lot of clichéd movies.

Part 2

I spend a great deal of energy planning every step my shoes take, and I don't do that for my own amusement. I do it because while the world repeatedly reminds me that it cannot be controlled, I want to have complete control over my decisions.

Since that day in '88, I've lost some of that control every time someone blamed a drunk driver, a poorly designed street, bad brakes on a truck, or God. It puts me in a position where I am forced to ask some other entity why they did what they did, and I am forced to acknowledge that it could happen again. How could I possibly plan if I couldn't manage, understand, and control all the variables?

Even more crucially, the effort I expend for whoever's ascribing the blame in the moment is just as wasteful as the anger I'd feel toward the entity to whom blame is ascribed. Those who ask the question will leave for their next event and those I blame can't, or won't, ever hear or care anymore. And when I fret about the weight of the question or statement or rail at the consequences of someone's ill-thought-out actions, that energy spent is mine alone.

That act of assigning blame takes an already asymmetric relationship between someone else and me and tilts the balance of ownership overwhelmingly in their favor. And that I can't sanction.

Don't get me wrong, I'm not completely immune to temptation. I am at least half-human, after all.

I've done poorly in classes and convinced myself that an illness was to blame.

I've skipped meetings in other buildings by convincing myself that walking between them was too hard and, you know, maybe if I could walk as quickly as the others ...

I've asked for special treatment blaming everything from my crutches to the weather.

The only saving grace is that when I slip into that mode, I'm reminded of the whiny child I've tried to avoid being since that day in '88. Being that child means getting the security blanket of blaming others. And while it may reveal the human parts sitting in the prostheses, it hurts those around me who have tried their best to help me avoid that easy way out.

When others do try to offer the easy way out, my family's faces are a mix of tight smiles and studied politeness as they retort: "His two crutches are enough; don't give him more."

I will never really have a better answer than that one; it's been over thirty years, and the most effective solution for me is still to take responsibility for my decisions and identify the factors that give me the most agency. At the very least, it restores the symmetry of my relationships with others. The energy I spend is all mine again, to direct where I choose.

Perhaps this approach involves too much self-criticism, but it's a worthwhile risk for someone like me who can see their petulance in the corner of every mirror. Fundamentally, if the problem is loss of agency and the goal is regaining it, this act of taking responsibility brings the act of solving within my control as well.

The "Why would God do this?" question completely bypasses my need for some measure of agency over my life. Regrettably, I cannot afford the luxury of reducing my challenges to a rhetorical flourish. I'll always need to conserve my time and energy to constantly re-learn how to stand and walk instead of participating in ritual blaming. I've already been there and have worked out that I can no more talk to God than I can control the weather; equally, I can no more damn drivers of disagreeable vehicles than I can control friction.

I can, however, stay indoors when it snows, buy crutches that don't slip in the rain, watch for heavy traffic, or get a ride if all else fails.

Maybe someday I'll throw caution to the wind and skip all those precautions, and if so, I'll have only myself to blame.

Till then, I can enjoy the earnest questions of strangers in the elevator who ask, with complete innocence, whether I'd hurt myself skiing over the weekend.

YOU

Is 197 a prime number?

Maybe you know the answer, maybe you don't. Either way, you're probably thinking, What does that have to do with anything? And if you are, I've succeeded at my goal when a typical conversation starts—I've distracted you away from the line of thinking that began when you first saw me.

And now that I've pointed it out, it's back again, isn't it?

Funny how that happens.

You see, when people see or talk to someone like me, the first thought overwhelming their mind is either the one telling them to be respectful or the one telling them not to be patronizing.

They imagine that I've somehow gone all these years without having noticed my disability and worry that they might accidentally point it out to me.

That leaves me with two options, the first of which is aggressively pointing out the elephant in the room to get things over with. That doesn't improve the conversation because our collective awareness of the elephant reminds us how big it is and how small the room has become.

The second and far more comfortable option—in my experience—is moving to a different room altogether, preferably one with less space taken up by wildlife. We can then talk without either of us overthinking our sentences in a desperate attempt to find the right words to say.

Neat, right?

I learned this approach from one of my favorite perches: any place within earshot of Ma talking to someone.

Ma has this uncanny ability to put anyone—and I mean anyone—at ease. She can walk up to a total stranger and leave minutes later, having made a new friend. There are people whom she has met twice who, upon recognizing her, talk to her like she's known them all their lives. Kids she taught decades ago still remember and adore her. She's the one person in our family that every one of our neighbors knows, and every one of their pets loves. Cats who hate human contact will cuddle at her feet; dogs that growl at everybody will wag their tails and lick her palms. There is a mob of crows near our flat that remains convinced, to this day, that she is the only one in the entire human race who has access to food.

There are those who can hold a conversation on any subject, anytime, anywhere, and we marvel at their talent. Ma's super-power is just as marvelous: she will convince you that you're one of those talented few.

"Ma, I have to move it there; otherwise, it will lock."

"No, if you twist it that much, you'll hit the one on your left."

"Yes, but I can't just lift the left leg! It's going to hurt on the right leg!"

"All right, but you're wrong, and when…. Ha! Told you! Do you need my help standing up, or do you want to do that your way too?"

I don't remember the first time Ma taught me to walk, but I do remember the second time. We had purchased some heavy wooden shoulder-height crutches, and she was trying to get me to transfer my weight correctly. A young friend of mine was hanging out with us, and after about the third time I fell, she commented that maybe if I used a single crutch and someone else's shoulder for balance, I'd feel more stable. That did make more sense, I nodded eagerly, but Ma wouldn't budge.

We tried for fifteen more minutes, and I got slightly better before falling again. I begged Ma to try the single-crutch approach, and she reluctantly conceded. About three minutes after my friend and I high-fived to celebrate having convinced an adult, I tripped her and then myself, and we landed unceremoniously on the floor.

Ma shook her head and added, "Nice try. Let's try with two crutches. One day, she's not going to be there, and I'm not going to be there, and you're still going to need to get somewhere. Now, up!" And we practiced for another forty-five minutes.

It took me some time to get comfortable sitting in a wheelchair for long durations, but once I did, my favorite position was parked just outside the kitchen while Ma was in there.

Weekday mornings were always chaotic, and the kitchen was the eye of the hurricane. Dee would be yelling from behind me just to let Ma make breakfast, or she'd be late for school. Appa would be just about finishing up his prayers and pause to grimly shake his head at the madness around him. Our driver, who needed to show up at 7:20 AM to take Ma and me to school, would amble in about twenty minutes late rehearsing his excuses. And through it all, Ma and I would be chatting about the latest movie we both hated as she raced from one utensil to another and I chomped on some toast.

"Ma, you've already added salt to that one …"

"No, I haven't, not to this one. I added some to the other one …"

"No! That's this one; you've now added salt twice!"

"You're wrong. And even if I did, salt is good for you … probably. Now, what was that movie with …?"

As bad as this chaos sounds, there is one thing that could reliably make it worse: rain. Buses would be infrequent, streets would be crowded with honking cars and irate pedestrians, and our driver would be missing in action. The stairs weren't easy to navigate on these days, and we'll get to why in a bit; for now, know that on rainy days like these, I waited for a grown-up to join me on the trip downstairs.

On one such occasion, Ma was getting increasingly worried that our driver wouldn't show up and eventually decided that I should head downstairs. We'd figure out a plan, she told me, and she'd hail some auto-rickshaw nearby.

As we negotiated our way down the stairs, we ran into one of the neighbors who offered to give us a ride to school. I looked at the rain pouring down, weighed the relative comfort of this kindly gentleman's offer, and recalled my initial attempts at walking.

This is what my training was about all those years ago! I thought. Even if he weren't there, I'd still need to get to school so we should do this on our own.

Before Ma could say a word, I interjected a brusque "No, thanks!" and stalked off, proud of my independence. An hour later, drenched from the downpour, we had finally managed to get into an auto-rickshaw, and I avoided eye contact as Ma grumbled about how stupid I'd been.

Back home, I could always look forward to another chaotic morning and another movie debate.

"Ma, this is the same actor who was also in that other movie!"

"Mm-hmm. No, it isn't."

"But you don't even know which movie I'm thinking of!"

"Yes, I do! And you're wrong! But first, go put these plates on the table …"

A few years after that rainy school day, we were on our way back from Kolkata (then Calcutta). It'd been a fun trip away with family, but after a week of crashing around with cousins

I'd started to miss Delhi. The train journey back would take a while, but still, I knew that anticipating home would help alleviate the boredom. Till we discovered our seats and found that instead of a single cabin with berths for the four of us, we had two in one cabin and two in another.

As Dee prepared to clamber upstairs to check out her berth, and Appa muttered under his breath about the wisdom of the Indian Railways, Ma seemingly vanished. We could hear her voice coming from somewhere in the coach car and see the bobbing head of her brother nearby, but we couldn't spot her anywhere.

Sometime later, Ma emerged triumphantly from two cabins down and pointed our cabin out to a group of college undergrads. Apparently, their group had been separated by our booking, and Ma had advised them of a convenient trade whereby we'd get their cabin, and they could be seated closer to their group in ours. Watching Ma guide Appa and Dee to the other cabin, heavy bags in tow, my uncle admiringly observed, "Your mother could talk anyone into doing anything, you know. I don't think she even knew they were all one group, and now they think it was their idea!"

Twenty years after uncle described Ma that way, it's as true today as it was then. For just as long, I've wanted to pick up some part of that skill. Ma befriends people so naturally that you wouldn't even notice how much you'd told her.

Meanwhile, every time I talk to someone my mind races to find the next sentence that might somehow distract from the glaring reality of my crutches. Those same crutches that, despite their intended goal of independence, mostly scream a need for help.

Remember I told you before about stairs being a problem? You see, I use two elbow crutches when I walk, one for each arm, but I, ahem, gracefully downgrade from that when going up or down staircases. Most staircases have narrow steps with banisters, and it's just simpler to negotiate those with a single crutch. It almost always works, except for those artsy, narrow spiral ones or the ones in parks with wider steps and sloping greenery in place of banisters on either side; they have my permission to go straight to hell.

Conveniently, of the thirty-two steps between our flat in Delhi and the ground, twenty-eight are narrow and have banisters. There's a landing at each floor and between floors, and while the staircase turns, it never curves. I've gone up and down that staircase for almost twenty years, sometimes racing down as fast as I could, sometimes idly whistling to myself, thinking about nothing at all. I've had to step around potted plants, delivery people with large packages, and even excitable kids with their exasperated grandparents following behind.

That staircase prepared me for every single staircase I've climbed since, and I know it well. The main challenge is those last four steps at the end when it rains. They're narrow and have no banister, just the flush building wall, and they, too, have my permission to go straight to hell.

When a neighbor once told us that they'd contracted construction workers to build a banister for those last four steps, I hastened to point out how unnecessary that was, and that I'd managed just fine without any support. They noted then, with some amusement, that they'd had their elderly mother in mind, not just me. It had never even occurred to me that other people could benefit from banisters too.

Far too many of my conversations have begun at the top of a stairwell, with someone asking me if I needed assistance or directing me to the elevator. If I took their arm, I'd have company, and perhaps my walk would be easier. But surely there would come a day when they weren't around.

Isn't the goal doing it on my own, solving it on my own, and being on my own? Am I not supposed to move, to grow as quickly as possible, to help others instead of asking for them to help me? Or better yet, to steer them in such a way that they don't need me either?

These are certainly conclusions you'd expect from someone who believed that they'd survive perfectly well without help and, when they received some, thought they'd deserved it anyway. Someone who, after giving the self-important speech about "You won't always be there," also had to listen to, "Yes, but while I'm here, let me help."

Ma's gifts include many things. Things like easing into conversations; asking for help and planning backup contingencies when help isn't available; balancing some great options and some bad options to help find everyone a good option; knowing when to, with whom, and how often to talk.

But she has also taught me that pride in your independence can descend very easily into vanity; that self-reliance is four short yet dangerous steps away from self-involvement; that distraction is often the most efficient form of honesty; that it's not always about us and we just need to shut up; that people offering help are just trying to start a conversation too.

That picking random trivia about staircases and talking about it helps every other issue, every other pain, every challenge in the world to simply dissolve away.

Oh, and by the way, 197 is indeed a prime number.

ME

Every narrative about disability starts with essentially the same first chapter. The sort where the beloved protagonist starts off with troubles and tries to fight them off single-handedly. Eventually, they realize their error, combine their strengths with those around them, and win gallantly in the end. It is moving, it is inspirational, it is so, so very powerful.

And yet, in my case, it would've been an utter and complete lie.

Don't get me wrong, the people I mention in these pages do exist, and the conversations, while from memory, are largely accurate. However, if I only wrote a heroic description of myself, I'd never hear the end of it from the people in my life.

So, here's the realistic version.

Imagine you're just a small child and you've been rudely thrust into a new reality as I was. For the next few days after the inciting event, everyone around you twists themselves into knots to avoid upsetting you. Incidentally, the doctors, surgeons, and rehabilitation therapists are probably the frankest lot you'll meet, even if it takes you years to understand what they're saying.

But the challenge comes from the other well-meaning folk who are struggling to process the event and the outcome themselves. And in their haste to put you (and themselves) at ease, they forget that recovery from such an event and living with a physical disability doesn't dim the ego, the cynicism, or the selfishness inherent in all human beings. If anything, it takes everyone around you to make sure those qualities don't take over.

Everybody around you instinctively says, "We don't want to single you out; we want to treat you just like everyone else." But it's unlikely that they themselves believe it will happen.

Then, let's say some time has passed. You're home from the hospital and one day you stubbornly refuse to drink your milk. You even try to dump it on the floor. Would you expect your parents to scold you? And what about if you did this while sitting in a wheelchair? If you're really, truly, honest about wishing to be treated like any other kid, then the wheelchair shouldn't be part of the equation at all.

I'm relieved to say my family got this concept quickly, and after some early misbehavior I made sure never to test their resolve again.

However, this desire to normalize my childhood as much as possible came with caveats. My family, for example, worked hard to ensure that I didn't take the words "special assistance" for granted.

Years later, when friends wait patiently while I insist on taking the stairs, I expect a reaction that is equal parts admiration and annoyance. And rather than pretending it's all okay, I expect absolute candor from those friends. Anything less and the resentment might fester and come out in other ways.

Put another way, equal treatment for me can only occur if I also expect to be treated as kindly or harshly as anyone else. I've been very, very lucky to have everyone around me who behaved this way from the start.

Yet every single person, at some point, must go through a rebellious phase when something inside them wants to break the rules to see what happens. So, despite my parents' best attempts, I still managed to sneak by with some hideous episodes. (Which is just testament to how big an ass someone can be if they're allowed.)

Imagine that little child version of you has now grown into a teenager in high school. Assume that you could only walk with one crutch and needed the assistance of someone to get around. Assume further that some meet-and-greet that you desperately wanted could not occur without the approval of the school principal. But the principal is unavailable, and no other classmate would be available to take you along, so you decide to cut class and head out on your own, knowing that you may fall with no one to help in the corridors, on the stairs, or even on the floors in front of the office you target.

Your powers of inducing guilt are nascent, but your imagined powers of balance and forethought are absolute. You reach said offices, still get rejected, head back, and try to sneak back into class (a difficult task, in general, but still harder with a metallic crutch). Since you're lucky, you get a parental scolding not just for skipping class and acting like a yahoo but also because any of those falls could've been really bad.

Here's another hypothetical example. Your parents, recognizing the fragility of the engineering on which your health and education rests, have negotiated with the teaching staff some privileges like an emergency pick-up. Emergencies have happened once or twice before, warranting such a setup, and the emphasis is on the word "emergency" rather than on "pick-up."

Assume that your teenage self has left some homework at home that your addled brain has decided is important (that's the genius of it, in some ways; it's important after it was missed but not important enough to have ensured its presence in the first place). You realize only your sister is at home studying and that your mother is at work teaching but choose to elevate the urgency of your need. That grade is suddenly deemed a must-have. You conveniently edit out the "emergency" part in your head and make the call asking for a drop-off of the homework.

Alarm bells go off at home a few miles away, which then leads to a call at some workplaces, and a parent shows up to hand over said homework with a gritted smile. That evening at dinner you endure a tense silence in which you are locked out of conversation.

In my case, I was lucky that at the end of dinner, the silence was broken simply with a single, pained question: "What if this had been a real emergency and no one was available?"

These examples seem nothing more than a child acting up. And yet, I mention these events (not hypotheticals, you may have noticed) because there is no outcome where I could've really won.

The class-skipping expedition ended in failure, but more importantly, every stair I took and every step I walked could've ended with a painful fall. The homework grandstanding was (under a broad definition) successful, but the runaround that I had caused potentially made every future "emergency" call meaningless. So why plow on when some quiet, rational part of your brain recognizes the lose-lose situation and is insistently trying to convince the rest?

Simple. If the general population has given you the errone-ous impression that the mere existence of your disability grants you a bonus of social capital, and you've decided that rules are for the less worthy, why the hell would you not try to game the system? This then leads down a path where you don't even attempt to earn generosity because you've cultivated the belief that you're owed everyone's kindness. Then, later on, when someone doesn't mentally genuflect and outwardly admire the "high cost" that you've decided you've paid, the soothing breeze of cynicism can waft in, placing them squarely in the wrong.

Hence, the intentional disregard of any stresses that the family encounters.

Hence, the deliberate ignorance of the cost your friends must pay for the social capital you've squandered.

Hence, the immediate tears at the slightest hint of perceived pain.

It takes a while to peer through that cloud of self-involvement and learn that those who care don't only see what is; they also see the risks involved.

That one incorrect step on a staircase could lead to a far more serious injury.

That when a phone call to understand an absence past mid-night goes unanswered, the train of worry starts at, "I hope he's safe" but quickly heads to, "What if some joint on the left leg broke?"

And when an email from a friend reads, "It's been almost a week since we met for lunch," in between the lines hides a far worse fear.

Not knowing the fears others live with, it's tempting to think that they're just getting in the way of your well-deserved and infinite supply of fun.

If you're willing and eager to ignore the expressions of concern from those around you, it can be quite the party. And I kept partying on for quite some time, despite other smart kids topping me in class (when I begged God to make me smarter as compensation for lost physical faculties); despite the friends who left (and came back only when the whining stopped); despite the first two years of university (where no amount of moaning over physical exertion would matter in exams requiring mental agility).

It was so all-consumingly glorious that it led me all the way into year three of university when I marched up to my parents and told them I had planned out my entire life. Each questioning pinprick that followed from them served only to make me realize that this planning wasn't mine alone and the party balloons didn't deflate so much as they exploded. I've often thought back to those moments, and to this day the recollection is enough to make my prosthetic toes curl. Some self examination was hard but necessary because it forced me to acknowledge how far I'd stretched the limits of affection, patience, and comfort; every inch I'd been given on account of my disability had become a mile I started to demand.

I knew I'd always be planning the parameters within which my life would work, but this self-reflection forced me to realize how short-sighted and self-centered my plans were.

There's a distinct difference between the good kind of selfishness and the bad kind. My battle always has been against slipping into the wrong kind. So even as I recognized that I would always need to look out for myself, I was also reminded that if I need to be somewhere I won't get there by shoving friends and family around.

Especially when they tap me on the shoulder and point out I'm going the wrong way.

WORDS

I must've been in Class 10 or 11, and it was among the first opportunities I received to show off what six years of staring at a computer screen had earned me. Up until then, I could only find ways to bore classmates and annoy teachers, but apparently, on this occasion, there was a visitor from the Nehru Planetarium who had no reason to suspect how much of a geek I was.

Our school was holding some sort of science exhibition, and after a few weeks of messing about with web design, I had cooked up a mini-website devoted to publicly available images from the Hubble and of other suitably spacey-looking things.

In all honesty, the images themselves didn't matter, but the pages were, in my estimation, hyperlinked perfectly. When I did demonstrate it to teachers, the computer-literate among them were impressed (seeing as it was 1999) while the rest just saw some awe-inspiring pictures.

When, finally, our special visitor showed up, surrounded by a crowd, she briskly noted that one picture was of the Eagle Nebula, that another of the Sun was taken from some particular satellite, and that the project overall was a good beginning and an interesting idea. I remember being impressed at her visual recall, relieved that nothing had abruptly broken, but also irrationally disappointed that no one cared that this involved both HTML and Perl and was not your average Windows application.

A few days later, a neighbor told Ma that she had been quite impressed to see my name getting some attention in the newspaper. Ma excitedly came back and told the rest of us that perhaps the presence of someone from the Planetarium had drawn the press, and we should try to find the snippet.

That afternoon we pored over the last few days' newspapers. But after thirty minutes of hunting and only a sprinkling of local news articles, we came up empty. Appa pointed out that maybe they bought a different daily newspaper, and we should ask them for their copy. Over a phone call, the neighbor told us that they got the same newspaper as us and added the precise date and the page number. A few frantic minutes passed before we found it and I read it out loud.

"… Three participants, one of them disabled, displayed some computer applications …"

That's a bit dismissive, I thought; parts of my code were quite novel, and the description made it sound like it was no greater than a child's science experiment.

As I started to set the paper down, I commented, "That's a bit rude …" and noticed that Appa was frowning. Then he got up and stalked off.

Worried, I went over to Ma and asked, "Is he disappointed that they didn't describe it in more detail? Maybe they just don't understand what a website is."

"No, that isn't it," she sighed, "He's upset because he thinks you're upset at their use of the word disabled."

Apparently, getting upset is contagious; now I was angry and upset that Appa was upset on my behalf. And all because of some artlessly phrased text in a tiny article.

Dinner passed, as did the night, and life carried on. But at some point, during the next few months, the reality hit me: despite years of work at fitting in, I was still noted and defined as "disabled." A journalist could use that descriptor, and a casual neighborly reader without any other context would be able to pinpoint that the one-word descriptor was about me.

Sixteen years of life, eleven years of work, three schools, and two prostheses—all reduced to one word, which summarized nothing and subtracted everything.

In a perverse desire to find an alternative synonym, something that wouldn't take so much away, I pecked my way across the lone dictionary we had. (I still love the fact that while novels with swear words—or, shall we say, aggressively romantic words—were kept on shelves higher up and away from me, a dictionary with detailed descriptions of all those words remained within arm's reach.) "Incapacitated" and "crippled" seemed far worse and made it sound like my condition was considerably more ominous than it really was.

I was barely sixteen and the novels I did read—the ones on lower shelves—used words like "infirm" or "invalid" for their eighty-year-old characters. That left two, but both "handi-capped" and "disadvantaged" made me cringe because of the implied difficulty. Reluctantly, I concluded that I was stuck with "disabled" after all.

Remember, this was the late 90s and like many others, I was envel-oped in the assumption that the US would have a solution for this word problem. It seemed like snappy, minimalistic descriptors were always emerging (even if they were verging on the politically incorrect). You know how they say it's always dangerous to meet your idols because they could disappoint? I realized that years later when during a fire drill in my dorm room in Providence, I found myself having to request help with the stairs owing to my "mobility disability." So much for snappy minimalism.

Regardless, let's return to the 90s for a bit. It's a minor struggle for me to describe why those words annoyed me so much. It's not like I was teased for the way I walked. And despite the various cliques in our school, I was more likely to be teased by close friends for being too smart, too nerdy, or too fat, than I was for my crutches. Far from being a loner glowering in the corner of the cafeteria, my friends and I had so much fun pretending my crutches were guns as we "hunted" each other that we were all scolded about the expense of new crutches and the trouble I'd have if they'd been broken.

But what annoyed me was that words like disabled separated me from my friends. If you wanted to say that one of us was an athlete, the other was literary, the third was a maths whiz, and so on, leaving me out by elimination, I would understand and would find a way to compete. But the artlessness of those words is that they tell me that my friends have something I don't have and never will have.

Try pointing out to a teenager that there's something they don't have and that, because of it, they'll never fit in. See how well that goes over.

The converse is true, too, and somehow the "positive" labels become even more reductive and galling. For every instance I've stood in a queue for the handicapped or been recommended to use a parking spot for the disabled, there's someone telling me how "brave" I am.

And yes, I have persevered in the face of difficulties. But I'm not alone.

For example, in my day job I am surrounded by people working with at times limited, poorly defined data given to them by other, very harried coworkers and still somehow finding a way forward.

And, of course, in the last three decades, I've met several doctors guiding some incredibly sick people to recovery, often in the face of those same patients wanting to give up.

But I'd say those coworkers and doctors have agility, leadership, and persistence rather than reducing their qualities to bravery alone.

Therein lies the problem. Reduction to a token negative like "disabled" is no better than reduction to a token positive like "brave"—the first constructs an obstacle that can't be overcome, and the second presumes an indefatigable spirit to conquer the same obstacle. Surely, a rational mind would tell us, if one is impossible, the second must be as well.

But without the expense of analysis, a soundbite does nicely for those in charge. It's also how I can graduate from the "handicapped boy" in our neighborhood to the "brave, handicapped child" in my school to the "brave, disabled person" in the US. And as if that weren't enough to make one gag, during a vacation I saw a news item describing someone as "differently abled." Does it hurt to bend over backward that much? Or is it massaged away by the feeling that it's a sincere attempt in an aw-shucks kind of way and, therefore, not utterly ridiculous?

Is there any harm in reclaiming the words of normal conversation instead of these contrivances? Are we that willing to default to political correctness that we're okay with the resulting tedium?

The grammar of disability in the words I read is nothing like my actual life where I wear my prosthetics because, as my niece likes to say, a long time ago, I broke my legs. And when my walking isn't stable, those closest to me refer to it as hobbling around to acknowledge that my stride is not as comfortable as it could be.

In the middle of an argument at grad school, I casually pointed out to my friend that, in my expert opinion, he "didn't have a leg to stand on." You know when there's uproarious laughter that you've graduated from being the punchline to the satisfying experience of deploying one.

People who don't know me will always notice first what I don't have, can't do, or won't be. And truthfully, there are a lot of areas where I will never quite be good enough.

I can be professional, but I can never have the work ethic Appa has.

I can be strong, but I will never be as strong as Ma is.

I can be skilled, but never as much as Dee or Jeej are.

I can be creative, but not as much as my niece already is.

I can be patient and caring and thoughtful, but never as much as my friends have been.

Over time, I've experienced the highs of accomplishment and managed to ignore the slight tinges of how those accomplishments are sometimes characterized. It's tempting at these points to swing around and criticize (as Dee is wont to do), but it's still wasteful; reductive attempts at categorization can change but not always on the whims of individuals.

Now, at my day job, I'm frequently discouraged from stating problems without solutions, so allow me to suggest a different word.

There's a Hindi colloquialism, jugaad, that sums up a fix, a life hack, an improvisation, a bending of the rules to solve something intractable. That's the best description I've found for how we can approach a situation for which we aren't given an instruction manual or even the right vocabulary. When there are no well-defined rules, all you can do is improvise.

That's how I wish to be referenced: not "disabled" or "handicapped" but a life hacker. Someone who has worked hard to take his environment as it is and adapt it in creative ways to get on.

Part 3

"I judge you unfortunate because you have never lived through misfortune. You have passed through life without an opponent—no one can ever know what you are capable of, not even you."

— Seneca

"Your arguments are irrefutable. I am R. Daneel Olivaw. The 'R' stands for 'robot.'"

— Isaac Asimov, Prelude to Foundation

NORMAL

There are two established truths in our family. The first is that Appa has a fantastic sense of direction, and we thank God for that because the second truth is that he enjoys his walks. Awful weather, crowded streets, oncoming traffic, potholes, and long distances could form a grand alliance and still be, at best, a minor inconvenience to any stroll Appa devises for himself.

Conveniently, it is also the easiest way for me to break in a new set of legs. For every set I've had, Appa has identified their breaking point long before I have.

The objective of the walk is to combine conversation with experimentation. "Am I balancing weight correctly? Is my stride long enough to give me speed but not so long that I'll fall?" And on and on, it goes. It would be disrespectful of me to call Appa names but let's be honest—you can take a nerd out of engineering, but you can't take engineering out of a nerd.

Once, needing a haircut, I was convinced to go on a walk to a barbershop some distance away. I say convinced because I hadn't walked that far in a while, and the only argument in favor of this plan was that Appa knew of a shortcut. Doubt could've set in, but I refer you to Truth One regarding Appa's sense of direction. So, we set off, and after nearly twenty-five minutes of walking from him and huffing from me, we were halfway there.

"We're really close to the shortcut; you'll see how much time it saves," he said.

Five minutes later, he gestured proudly at an approaching gate. With a flourish, he unhooks the gate from its latch, we walk through, he latches it back on, and we walk on … for another twenty minutes.

"That was the shortcut?" I asked with about as much exasperation as I could muster through panting breaths.

He responded, "Yes! And now we only have to cross the street once!"

Incidentally, he complains when he's reminded of this story, but not more than I do, and here's why. After the haircut, I'd regained enough energy to grumble about how utterly useless his shortcut was. And in the interests of ensuring a fair comparison so that I'd "appreciate the merits of the shortcut" (his words, not mine, although it was hard to miss the glee on his face) Appa decided that we'd take the longer way back on our walk home.

What makes dealing with this kind of underhandedness worthwhile is our family's amusement at observing Appa's gait; you can't miss it once I tell you why. It's not just the short, measured steps, it's not just the bolt upright posture, and it's certainly not just the head facing forwards at every instance except intersections. What really makes it an art form is the bounce.

That tiny bounce at every step! It doesn't matter if he's happy, if he's angry, or if he's upset … the bounce stays! That bounce is Appa in a nutshell: it doesn't matter if he's troubled or not; he wants to make sure that he doesn't trouble even the pavement underneath him.

Appa is a firm believer in being independent. He may be more aware of the help he's received than anyone I know, but he fully subscribes to the idea that you're handed nothing and earn everything. There've been many times when this streak of independence (which Dee and I have inherited) has roughed up feathers. But you can't draw a line from a flat in Delhi to an apartment in Redmond without recognizing that inherited streak.

When I was a child, this desire for independence felt laughably unnecessary. My family was always around, and I assumed they'd always be around; planning for a future on my own seemed nonsensical. For them, however, encouraging my independence was a solution to the constant whys and hows that surround a disability.

From a very early age, the point was never "You should do it by yourself" or even "You must do it by yourself," but "You can do it by yourself, just like everyone else does." That's the bar: normalcy.

Society is designed for normalcy. Our shelves are designed at the "average" height; our houses are designed for the "average" family; what we wear, what we drive, where we work, and how we fall in love, all of it is designed for the perfectly normal. We may customize when absolutely necessary or extend "privileges," or even celebrate others in "special" events. But the cost of that inclusivity never goes unseen. (At the same time, we charmingly wonder at what point "average" came to mean the same as mundane and boring. But I digress.)

None of this mattered when I was six because I was still at school and still playing cricket with friends. I got into trouble just like them and took the stairs two floors to our flat just like everyone else. Whenever I was called freakish at school, it was because I did well in class and not because I couldn't join in during gymnastics lessons. Maybe I was too young to be concerned.

In the teenage years, insecurities creep in. You begin to wish you could stay the night at your friends' house but immediately dismiss it as logistically infeasible. Or you wish that they could stay over at yours but worry about what they'll think when the legs come off. (That inner monologue of defeatism is so loud that you even miss it when they say "Yes! Of course!" and need to have it repeated back to you.)

In a weird way, that fear of rejection and constant overthinking made even my teenage rebellions mind-numbingly normal.

I didn't smoke, drink, or otherwise get into trouble; in fact, I couldn't even if wanted to, not when doing any of those things required putting on my legs, taking the stairs, and a walk to the shops or to the park behind the shops. Worrying about falling was probably more effective against that slippery slope than family values. I think I'd have preferred to get slapped for asking Ma to buy me a packet of cigarettes on her next visit to the grocery store than for taking up smoking at all.

My restless teenage energy was spent on a vigorous chase of academic success. If I was going to be a loner, I was going to be an elite one. That'll weed out those who never wanted me in any way, I thought, not realizing that I was projecting insecurity on people far more confident than I was.

That academic chase did have its good moments—the pleasant surprise of finding close friends, making it to university then grad school, and so on—but it lacked that certain indifferent coolness I wished I had. It's the classic immature schoolchild approach to problem-solving: mock something as much as you can, inadvertently revealing how much you want it.

It doesn't hit you when you're a child and too young to care, and it doesn't hit you when you're slightly older and too self-absorbed to notice. The consequence of years of ignorance followed by years of performed indifference is the weight of the albatross you're mightily trying to ignore. You acknowledge its existence every time you notice that you're pretending not to care again, and every time you do its weight on you grows.

But when you're surrounded by the right people, you eventually realize that there's no difference between trying to be normal, worrying about not being normal, and pretending you don't care about being normal—they're all equally exhausting.

Despite my exhausted fumbling in this regard, I was undeservedly lucky in my implementation. Friends around me didn't let me remain a loner and they absolutely didn't care about "indifferent coolness."

For example, when I was seventeen my left leg broke in two in a school hallway. The seven friends who surrounded me took this in stride and after getting me safely to a chair debated what tool from a Swiss Army knife might work on the knee joint in the absence of the necessary screwdriver. (The prosthetics specialist who eventually fixed me up was horrified, by the way, that a group of sec-ondary schoolers—egged on by yours truly—could've conceivably chosen to "repair" what he had carefully constructed.)

The point is that after much trying, worrying, and pretend-ing, I learned that "normal" is an illusory construct. It took me a while to figure that out, but what surprised me was how relieved I felt when it did.

The first time I felt that relief was when I began my under-grad studies, and I—like everyone else in my class—was over-whelmed by how much there was to do. The second time was in grad school when I stayed away from family and had to demonstrate—like so many other grad students—whether my parental training had really sunk in. And the third time was when—years after school was done—I went back to work after seeing my eleven-day-old niece quietly asleep in front of me.

I've learned that those who matter don't care that you're not like everyone else because they know they aren't either.

On those walks around the city with Appa in my teens and twenties, we talked about the importance of a green cover in a city, how economics and politics get intertwined, and even the physics of stress and strain. He said that the conversation helped distract me from focusing too much on the act of walking so that it felt more natural. He was right, of course. What he wanted was for my stride to be effortless and not forced.

Truthfully, I find that every single person, including myself, is at their most revealing when they walk.

When Ma starts making her way to, well, anywhere, it's with a sense of purpose and with the clear desire to make as much ground as quickly as possible.

On his strolls, Appa walks like he wants to get where he's going without bothering anyone along the way.

Dee and Jeej, as new parents, walk with a mix of frenzy and calm, as if they must defer their enjoyment of the journey till after they've hurriedly cleared out obstacles for their daughter.

Meanwhile, that niece whose baby pictures had pride of place at my home, skips the way I wish I still could—without fear, without purpose, and ignoring what the grown-ups tell her to do.

Either by instinct or by training, we don't watch ourselves walk, and that's why we never consciously try to walk "normally." Indeed, how we walk is the one thing we assume is accepted without question, just like we'd want ourselves to be.

And I walk like someone who's still figuring out where that next step goes.

TECH

Have you ever run into one of those couples who won't stop talking about how much they love each other, how great the love of their life is, and how they can't believe they've been together for so long? They barely notice your eyes glazing over and continue on and on. When they finally pause for breath it's only to gaze and sigh at each other, blissfully unaware that you've long since left the conversation.

Yeah, this is going to be a lot like that, so if that cloying chatter makes you ill, skip ahead.

Still here? Okay then, let me tell you about why I became an engineer.

Talking about tech is something of a challenge for me because of how deep that love goes. Some of it is to be expected—I work, after all, in Redmond and spend most of my day bathed in the light of a minimum of three screens and enveloped by the cloud. But what you don't readily see is the far more visceral reality. From the joints in my prosthetics to the service that delivers my groceries to the hand controls in the car I drive to work, that gentle touch of engineering is, for me, pervasive.

Thinking back, it was clearly meant to be. I have no idea if Ma and Appa realized how much getting a computer in the 90s would change things for me. Our family did always have an affection for the sciences, so maybe this was just a logical extension. Perhaps, they thought, it could be a skill or even a career when the inevitable job hunt arrived. Honestly, there could've been a hundred different whys and what-ifs, but as a software engineer, I've been schooled primarily in how, so let's start there.

Let's start with observing that the doctors and prosthetists who worked on me never talked down to the kid they were dealing with. And the way they approached getting me on my feet is the same way those in tech approach every problem they meet—with the excitement of finding a new challenge coupled with the belief that it can be understood and the thrill of finding a solution.

The first time I recognized that solution-finding thrill was in seeing grown-ups clap and cheer as I took my first step with artificial limbs. Years later, I felt it myself when I wrote my first program and saw those lines of code work. That first program was proof—if proof were even needed—that this interest in engineering was real, and it was worth pursuing.

That relentless optimism in tech was infectious enough that as time went on, I found I could forget everything else. Every awkward conversation, every vacant expression of pity, every bit of life's chaos faded once I touched the keyboard. All that remained was the puzzle I needed to figure out that day and whatever I could create to solve it. I was convinced then that this was much more than a flirtation; this was how I wanted to spend my life.

Much like any other teenage romance, I lost myself in my new obsession and left practicalities to everyone else. I knew I had to make this my career but gave no thought to how that would happen. Thankfully Dee, having gone through a similar phase with medicine and recognizing the signs, had ideas on what I should do.

So, it turned out, did Appa. As he's reminded me many times, his years in mechanical engineering have shown him how well nuts and bolts fit when the thread on each of them matches just so. But, he adds, you don't force that pairing; if you do and it doesn't fit, the thread will break and it will break for good.

The more I immersed in my chosen field, the more I discovered that the world of software development behaves as a community of equals.

In that world and on the Internet, nobody knows you're disabled.

None of the participants in conference calls care about the number of hydraulic joints in the room.

None of the users of products I've built concerned themselves with whether the engineer needed crutches to get around.

And none of the teams I've worked on concerned themselves with my physical disability because the only thing that mattered was whether I had the ability to get things done.

Naturally, I've developed an appreciation for the advantages this industry has brought me. It's evident that at one level I would not have a career, a way to contribute and to prove myself. If it weren't for what that egalitarian virtual world offered, I wouldn't even be out in the real one.

And once I entered the world of professional engineering, it became obvious that I held another unique advantage. Capable engineers acquire a vast array of techniques from years of study and on-the-job learning. But while everything most engineers learn is from training, everything I know is through pure instinct developed from walking. Their skill might atrophy and fade from disuse, but I won't—I can't—forget watching where I walk and preparing for when I fall. The accidental anonymity of tech had created a refreshingly level playing field, and a lifetime of experience had finally found utility in a career.

In addition to this, my mental toolkit has two important tools in it: one, the figuring out of rules in a system, and two, planning for when those rules break down. So, imagine my delight as I sat down at my desk on my first day at work and was told I'd be breaking things for a living.

However, this delight was quickly followed by dismay. I'd expected to start learning new things from my first day at work. But within weeks I discovered that if I was to be even slightly useful, I had to make fundamental changes to my own operating code.

Consider that all my training till now has been toward being independent and planning for myself. For years, I'd been trained to walk on my own, to explore by myself.

But that's just not how the tech industry operates.

Even if you could build a feature solo, it's hard to sustain a product by yourself. And when you're running a team, as I briefly did, you must depend on your team just as much as they depend on you. You never plan for yourself anymore, you simply can't. What you must do, however, is build what it takes to let others conceive their own plans and let their world rest comfortably on the turtles you've laid all the way down.

One idea central to my own construction has been that breaking something regularly is key to building it correctly. Whenever

I've learned to walk, I've fallen, and every time I fell, I learned how to walk better. From the bolts in my foot to the hairs on my head, I've been torn down and rebuilt so many times that I've adopted it not just as a programming style but as my programming itself.

But as an engineer I had to learn that when big things are delivered by teams, it's because they are improved incrementally, not constantly remade. In hindsight, the bug in the operating code seems obvious: I had always assigned risk analysis to every step I took, but, you see, new engineers never get the cost right.

A few years into my job (which now feels like such a long time ago), I had a long, drawn-out argument with an engineering manager—the lead of one of my partner teams—about how good code gets written. One side of the argument was all for starting immediately, making mistakes, failing fast, fixing, and learning as quickly as you can. The other side—perhaps more informed by experience—was about turning concepts into logical designs, framing logical designs as architecture, and finally, crystallizing architecture into code. The first argument favored lower costs at every step taken, and the second purported to lower risk over the entirety of the walk.

Unfortunately for both of us, I was too bull-headed to back away from the fight, and when he questioned my planning instincts, all I saw was red. My arguments with him were like playing chess with someone who already knows your best moves, so there are no points for guessing which side I argued or who won. What matters more is what he stressed that day (in increasingly exasperated tones) and what I've learned over the career that followed: writing complex, flexible, and scalable software is easier if you pause to design first. If your software is thoughtfully designed, the rest follows easily because it's simply implementation. (And when you don't force the bolt through, you don't break the thread).

Once you see the design alternatives, you realize that you don't solve disability with inspiration; you solve it with engineering. With that in mind, let's revisit what this engineering problem actually needs from us.

Despite going occasional loggerheads with coworkers, my love affair with engineering grows stronger each year. And from those early days of learning better teamwork skills, I've grown to integrate my foundational knowledge with all the rest. Here are some of the things I've come to understand in this field:

You're building for requirements you can't yet anticipate, so you need to be able to iterate and adapt often.

Mistakes and disruptions are expensive and may mean the difference between walking or falling.

You must recognize that reinvention is easy, but refactoring is incredibly hard.

Your design must be modular enough to change while in flight, and it must withstand constant and sustained usage.

And finally, but crucially, you'll almost always be standing with your hand on someone else's shoulder for support.

DECIDE

A beautiful thing about tech as a discipline and even as an industry, is how it has reframed laziness.

Most industries have a low tolerance threshold for laziness. But the tech industry doesn't merely endure or ignore this approach. If you can find a way to do something in one step instead of five or—even better—find a way not to do it at all, tech will celebrate your breakthrough, shower you with praise, and reward you with the euphemistic badge of "efficiency."

You can see why a constitutionally lazy person like me was bound to follow its siren song.

Before you begin to credit me with self-deprecation, allow me to elaborate.

When I was about eight or nine, one of my prosthetists saw me sweating and told me not to worry because amputees always burn more energy when walking, and my sweating was normal. I used that argument eighteen years later when explaining to my family why I couldn't put on weight and why they should just leave me alone about going to the gym.

I think you'll agree that viewed in that light, discovering an industry in which my lazy approach is celebrated is about the best thing that could've happened to me.

Here's another reason I take to tech: I live in my head the way athletes live in their limbs and actors live in their faces. And that means that I love puzzles, in whatever form they may take. They could be problem sets for an exam, they could be sequences of musical notes in a particular song, or they could be games, digital or not.

When a puzzle is particularly intricate and the solution slightly out of reach, I enjoy the resulting knot in my stomach. What matters to me is the hunt, and quite often, the solution will be beyond my grasp. On my good days, I'll get close to figuring it out, and on bad days, I'll be off by miles. But neither of those days hurts as much as when the puzzle is easily solved; I get bored very easily, and I hate puzzles that bore me.

So, it is convenient then that my day-to-day, with endless decisions, provides a steady supply of puzzles for my amusement.

For example, there is the technological puzzle of when and why parts of an artificial leg might shear. Then there is the physical puzzle whenever I'm unwell or in pain. At such times it's more comforting to remain in my head and figure out "fixes" while abstractedly surveying the rest of my screaming body. Engineers always feel more capable when they can visualize the system on which they work. It's far more challenging when you're the system in churn, which is, for me, an unavoidable factor.

However, in my constant puzzle-solving mode where body parts become systems and decisions become puzzles, finding fixes is complicated between two warring factions of my mind. The first is the restless faction that always wants something new to avoid boredom no matter how dangerous that might be. The second is the inertia faction that abhors risk, adores the status quo, and frequently reminds me that the lazy approach is an asset, especially while I'm on a particularly comfortable couch.

This tension between Restlessness and Inertia has persisted across every decision of my adult life as both factions try to dominate.

When I was growing up, neither faction could claim dominance. Besides the ongoing challenge of adjusting to new legs, there was no extraordinary puzzle I needed to solve. Going to school was a fait accompli, as were the classes I would take. I had no part in deciding which schools I would attend because I was too young or knew too little to choose. The few times in my later student years when I announced ambitious decisions,

I did so with sufficient incompetence that both factions of my brain agreed on a truce just to stay out of trouble. For most of what followed, my choices were winnowed down enough that what I did equated more to nodding than choosing.

Choosing Sanskrit or Hindi in Class 9? Dee took Sanskrit, so I would too.

Choosing science, commerce, or the humanities in Class 11? I'm only good at computers and nothing else, making it easy.

My university was chosen for its proximity, and grad school was decided upon due to procrastination (in line with the Magnificent Plan of Decision Avoidance).

By the time I was a young professional, I had absorbed the reality that decisions are fantastically easy to make when circumstances have already made them for you.

That truce among my mental factions continued amicably— the part craving laziness could wait for the solution, and the part craving action had an endless supply of mostly benign problems to feast on.

For example, work in Redmond began out of financial necessity, and the more I learned of my industry's favorable framing around laziness as "efficiency" and avoidance as "decision fatigue," the more I felt at home.

Decide

Peace in our time. Till it all fell apart.

Like every other war, this one also broke out due to something that should've been insignificant—it snowed.

On the face of it, this should have been an easy one. The streets and sidewalks were slippery, and I didn't have a car. I stayed home, as did most other people.

Two days went by, and Inertia, reveling in its sudden dominance, became complacent. Even as it kept me on schedule with meeting calls and meal orders, it failed to notice Restlessness sneaking in.

As Day Two ended and Day Three dawned, Restlessness gently suggested, "You should figure out how to walk in the snow by yourself." Fifteen minutes later, Restlessness had claimed a victory over Inertia, and I was outside.

Then both factions watched in horror as crutches slipped and knees buckled in unanticipated ways on an icy sidewalk. Inertia belatedly raced for control and held for another five minutes till it saw oncoming traffic and ran away screaming. I managed to find my way back inside. Still, more importantly, after both factions admitted defeat, a reluctant, risk-averse truce took hold between. But it felt nothing like the stable peace of before.

About five years later, the truce was broken and war broke out again. But this time over something more significant.

Until then, I had never paid any attention to my prosthetic upgrades; that had very much been Appa's domain, so I never bothered. I'd also had blisters and wounds on my leg before, and each time Inertia would prescribe a few days' rest.

Except this time, nothing ever fully healed, no matter how long I rested. I would spend a stretch of the week working from home, and by Sunday, everything would be fine; I'd leave for work on Monday and return home bleeding. I'd go in with a bandaged leg starting Tuesday, and blood would be everywhere on my right prosthetic by Friday.

Curiously, Restlessness was perfectly happy now that there was a harder problem to pick apart, and Inertia was thrilled as I repeated my cycle of bleed-and-rest for weeks on end.

Eventually, I succumbed and visited my prosthetist, who pointed out the obvious: a new set of limbs had to be made, and we needed to start on those soon, right here in Redmond. Recovery would be significantly faster that way.

This was not the biggest risk I'd ever taken and was certainly one with a worthy reward, but after the fall on the ice, even Restlessness didn't feel like gambling anymore. So, when the wound briefly healed, I flew out to Delhi to attend my niece's first birthday. While there, I told Appa that we should plan to make those new prosthetics in December when I visited Delhi again. I added that I hoped we could finish in my allotted three weeks off from work.

Appa asked me quietly if I thought that time frame was feasible based on our previous experiences. The answer—confirmed by my intuition—was no. It was a hateful answer, but also the right one. And I'd known it for almost four months.

I flew back to Redmond and spent December that year working long hours to stave off homesickness and iterating over prosthetics in whatever time remained.

The preparation of my prosthetics is possibly the most complex engineering process I'm involved in, simply due to the sheer number of decisions it requires. As a child, I'd always needed my parents to drive that process for me, but now, a young man working far from home, I'd had to do it on my own. It burned me out. I was upset at being away from family, but the bleeding stopped.

Despite my homesickness, I was now comfortable and secure in my Redmond life. And figuring out how to get my limbs made, made me feel more independent than ever. I had a place to live where I could reach the shelves, a job to go to where buttons opened doors and a car that I drove myself. I had friends I met for dinner and who'd known me for years, a pharmacy nearby with disabled parking privileges, and a gym I visited where trainers had programs specifically for me.

I became more familiar with the TV shows I watched in Redmond than the ones I had watched in Delhi. My dreams, that used to be in various languages, shifted to mostly English.

There were plenty of puzzles here to keep me occupied and lots of people to solve them with. I had the control I'd always wanted, yet despite all these factors I felt more indecisive than ever before.

Work in Redmond gave me problems to solve and a circle of friends and coworkers who taught me how to solve them, but it also gave me the means to fly back every year. Was this still going to be my pattern, I wondered, or were the strands tying me to my home in Delhi fraying beyond repair?

Whenever I see a problem, there's a voice in my head for every family member whose advice I rely upon.

I can consult the "Appa" voice for its rigor.

I can consult the "Ma" voice for its pragmatism.

I can consult the "Dee" voice for its diagnoses of whether I'm right or wrong.

But in this moment, those three voices in my head were in conflict. I clearly saw all the constraints, I knew what I wanted wasn't pragmatic, and there were no clear right or wrong answers.

Luckily, there's a fourth source of advice. This source trusts that I know how to decide but will advise me on why I need to decide soon. Whether it's a phone, a vacation, or tuition for grad school, I know that voice will cut through the chaff. So, when I flew to Delhi at the height of my indecision, I shared it out loud with Jeej. And I came back with some clarity on why I was battling indecision.

It's figuring out what that very first decision of mine will cost me.

A five-year-old running across the street does not see the costs of a disability. A five-year-old does not see the insecurity of a teenager who walks with crutches. Or the worry of a twenty-year-old pursuing an education and employment despite illness. Or the fear of a thirty-year-old that he might never enjoy love and companionship from anyone because they just see the limbs that are long gone.

Even as adults, it's impossible for us to see the future and the outcome of every possible path. And yet, time and time again, disability insists we make significant choices and demands a detailed accounting from us of not just every step but also the cost of those steps. Sometimes, when I'm really excited about where I'm going, I surrender myself to this accounting. On other occasions, I've chosen to spare myself the mental exertion. Either way, this assessment of the various paths I can take, their risk and their reward, remains a necessary but thoroughly exhausting activity for me.

No matter what, I eventually decided, the central strand would hold strong. Underneath it all, I wasn't Paris, Providence, or

Redmond; I was Delhi. It's where I could both revel in the laziness of Inertia and dare myself to enjoy Restlessness. It's where I began and where all my plans ended; where I begged to decide on my own, knowing I'd never have to. And I wanted to continue thinking of Delhi as home base not because it felt familiar or safe, but because it felt most like home.

Nowadays, I'm still committed to honing my efficiency skills, and coaxing Restlessness and Inertia to play nice with each other. But when I look at what's still unfinished from my list of things to do, they're not grand, sweeping puzzles anymore.

For instance, someday, after I've sat down in a park with someone I care about, I want to stand back up on my own.

Someday, when I go with my family to the temple, I want to not need them to untie my shoelaces for me.

Someday, I'd like to be more than a good student and grow into a fairly good teacher too.

I have no idea what it takes to cross these items off my list, but I've been training myself on strategies to get there. And that has been easier than I thought; the hard part, it turns out, was just deciding that I wanted to put them on the list in the first place.

CURIOUS

I was in my late twenties, and she was just a few days old.

It was the first time I saw someone smaller than me at home and as the previously youngest person in our family, finding someone new that I could boss around should've been a great moment.

But then Appa decided to go for a walk, and Dee needed a nap, and Ma told me she was going to take a shower and that I should keep an eye on this tiny bundle sleeping peacefully on the sofa beside me.

It should've been a great moment—I was finally in charge of someone else. I had reached those dizzying heights of adulthood that everyone talked about. After all, at that point, I had been through multiple exams of increasing difficulty across two degrees; I had been working for four years, and I was responsible for some rather complex tech. I considered myself, in all probability, to be on track to lead a team one day.

I was a verified, bona fide Grown-Up.

If you were to ask me today how long Ma was in the shower, I could not tell you. But I can tell you that approximately three dozen beads of sweat gathered on my forehead as I anxiously watched my sleeping niece. Every single one was a stinging reminder that while I thought I'd figured out how to manage myself impeccably, a nine-day-old sleeping bundle could dismantle me beyond belief.

A short time later, Ma showed up, picked her up, and took her into another room. Thankfully, she was too focused on her granddaughter to notice her son wiping his brow and sighing with relief.

Because you see, as I sat next to my sleeping niece, what I felt was something that I'd felt before. It happened on the first day of school, the first day at work, and the first time I met someone. That curious mixture of anticipation, dread, and insecurity all contained within one question: Do I really know what I'm doing?

Now, you might be inclined to think that this stress is unwarranted. As an uncle, I have the rare luxury of being both adored and redundant—frequently at the same time. Besides, I don't share any of her parents' responsibilities, and I don't see her as often as her grandparents do, so there really isn't any point in me sharing the stress.

A couple decades before my newborn niece arrived, not too long after I lost my limbs, one of our neighbors had a daughter. She and I were neighbors for several years (with our respective families, of course), and more than anything, someone that young meant I always had an audience to play-act with. My goofing around to make her laugh never went unnoticed. Even today, Ma remembers it with a smirk: "He's always been the youngest; I think he just wanted someone younger so he could be an older brother."

Ask any of the grown-ups, and they'll tell you that kids are very impressionable. Ma herself was very keen that my niece always have good memories of me from her childhood because she'll remember that time forever. I shrugged that off as so many words, till she came along to meet me at the airport at age three and started talking to me. She hasn't stopped since.

My friend and neighbor eventually moved out of Delhi and moved to another country altogether. We didn't see each other for several years till she visited us again, and I visited her at her house a few years after that. Neither one of us wanted to pretend (for reasons that will remain unexplained) that she was three again and I was a prancing horse; instead, we argued over the merits of the voting age and why I didn't take better care of my health despite having a doctor for a sister. And yet it is a matter of personal pride that in telling her about my hideously exaggerated travails at a hospital in Providence, I made her fall over laughing again.

My niece's birthday is in July, and so far, I've attended one of her birthday parties; my birthday is in December, and she's been to many more of mine. But to make up for that, whenever I'm in Delhi my time is her time. And her time is not for overthinking as much as I do. Halls in our flat can be traffic lights, traffic jams on the street can be conversation starters, and bouncy castles in amusement parks are just as much for me as they are for her. Why, you ask? She is growing every year and has progressed from looking up at me, to seeing eye to eye. When my limbs are off at home she behaves as though I'm smaller and must do as I'm told, not the other way around.

My childhood neighbor from Delhi is now my neighbor to the north. She's grown up faster than I did, is more self-aware than I am, and is more responsible and mature than I can hope to be. I had a six-year head start, and I can only watch in awe that someone to whom I taught both real and gibberish words has become insufferably more articulate than me. She'll one day find still more ways to heal people than she already does. But, far more importantly, I can still make her laugh.

Every time I see her, my growing niece doesn't just play with me or push me around; she thinks that she needs to look after me. Every time I prepare to return to Redmond, she worries how someone as incompetent as I am at being a Grown-Up will continue to survive. And in case you're wondering, I know this not because of my superhuman observational skills; she's told me this herself many, many times.

Her curious questioning doesn't bother me, and I'll tell you why. When kids ask about something unfamiliar, their questions come from curiosity and concern, not spite.

I've been stared at my whole life by doctors, by teachers, by strangers on the street; a child's stare, curious though it may be, is never as intrusive as that of the grown-ups that accompany them.

I've seen kids stare at me or wonder out loud, trying to figure out why this apparent human needs four legs. And when they do, they aren't told plainly that some of us need the help but are just fine in every other way; instead, they are scolded and embarrassed for having posed the question.

Is that really the virtue of being a Grown-Up, that we're allowed to stifle a question instead of answering it?

Ma never did. She told my niece what happened and that she must be careful crossing streets (Ma's good at turning uncomfortable questions into life lessons). In fact, having grown up trying to make people comfortable around us, my family has realized that it's far simpler just to feel comfortable within ourselves. We'd much rather be like these two girls in our lives; we'll share their glorious indifference to convention and their enthusiasm for events. We may be tactful like the Grown-Ups want us to be, but we won't exhaust ourselves thinking about what they might think of us.

When they were younger both shared the frankness that all kids are born with, and all adults deliberately stomp out. But neither showed the pity that somehow reliably streaks across the face of most grown-ups.

Both shared an affection for meeting new people and striking up chats like they'd known the other person for years. But neither looked at someone walking with crutches or sitting in a wheelchair and thought, "He can't play with us."

Both shared a worry less about the disability than they did about the general ineptitude of someone they were assured was older than them. And neither could hold back the giggles when this adult their size thought himself a dancer.

Two little girls. One who grew up and is still very much my little sister, and another who is little and fancies herself more grown-up than me. They were born almost twenty years apart, and yet, they couldn't be more alike, from their excitement to their exasperation.

It took a while, but I finally realized that kids don't participate in your world—they build a world where you happen to exist. And just like the other kids in our neighborhood, or the kids in my school, or the kids at the airport, I just wish we'd let them play.

Part 4

"He was the most inconsiderable creature in that swarming mass of mankind which for a brief space occupied the surface of the earth; and he was almighty because he had wrenched from chaos the secret of its nothingness."

– W. Somerset Maugham, Of Human Bondage

"When you have eliminated the impossible, whatever remains, however improbable, must be the truth."

– Arthur Conan Doyle, The Sign of Four

HELP

It was a roundish, silvery button with a blue icon on it and I'd never seen it before. It was near most, but not all, entryways at work. But staring at it awkwardly might be embarrassing, so I continued to walk past it as quickly as I could.

Later that day, I walked past it again, and no one was around, so I paused and stared more closely. I noticed a stylized wheelchair drawn on the button and that punching it opened the nearest door in a smooth swish.

Now, I'm familiar with doors and have walked through my fair share. Even so, I found myself quite impressed with the care being shown for those seated in a wheelchair—the doors were quite heavy, and it was a simple measure that made a lot of sense.

Years later, a coworker pointed out how much he appreciated my willingness to put in extra effort by noting how I never used the wheelchair access button and always pulled the door open, even though it must be hard. I rather sheepishly pointed out that I had always assumed they were reserved for wheelchair users and if I used it, it would probably be a social faux pas of some sort. He laughed off my protest, telling me not to be so self-deprecating, and I smilingly accepted his compliment.

The truth behind my smile is twofold—yes, I am that self-conscious of cultural and social missteps, but, more importantly, I've never needed that button because someone walking with me would always open the door for me. And to make it even worse, when they hadn't, or couldn't, there was a fetid corner of my brain that desperately wanted me to feel offended. After all, it thought, that's the least they could do.

Most of us hope we will leave enough of a mark over the course of our lives to be remembered by others. Yet in all honesty, we ourselves probably only have a fleeting memory of the large majority of people who've briefly passed through our own lives. And when we do remember those outside our closest friend and family circles, it is little beyond a moniker of their most affecting characteristic.

I realize this works both ways. So as much as I'd like that moniker for me not to be my disability, I am aware that it's the easiest thing to pick out in a crowd. In the last three decades,

I've gone from not realizing this to being aware of it, to being injured by it, and, finally, to being determined to change it.

Having that determination isn't hard, particularly considering how easy the problem actually is. Look at any movie, any TV series, or any book with a character that has a disability, and you'll recognize that displaying just one more dimension is sufficient to rescue the character from the stereotype.

This also works in real life.

For example, all I need to show is rudeness, selfishness, cheerfulness, or stupidity, and I can thoroughly circumvent that stereotype. Pfft, that's a walk in the park—I can do three of those on any given day.

Still, sometimes I prefer to adhere to an easy stereotype. It makes things so much simpler! All disabled people are expected to be unhappy, so if my walk to work tires me out enough to make me cranky, that is clearly to be expected. (Leave aside the fact that that kind of healthy exercise is the whole point of the prosthetics and the crutches.)

It makes it easier for everyone concerned if I fit neatly in that box. For example, if you calculate that because of the crutches, I shouldn't be expected to walk long distances, then I might calculate that knowing your calculations, I can ignore meeting you entirely because I wasn't expected to make it there anyway.

(Conveniently, since I'm expected to be an unhappy loner, I score a two-for-one—a clear win in every book.)

But then again, people like me are also supposed to be kind and wise, remember? And if you've read this far, you know I can find very, very creative ways to be selfish if needed. So, let's solve this problem differently. How about we still meet, but you walk over? I still don't walk any length whatsoever; I politely thank you for making the trip and wisely end up meeting you anyway. Surprisingly, you find I'm not really a cranky loner so we end up agreeing to meet where I work for future instances as well. That's an even better result—three birds with one hack!

Finding solutions to awkward social correctness has given me incredible satisfaction. It has allowed me to subvert the stereotypes in ways that bend the rules in my favor. You can and should fault me for preying on the kindness of others, but I can equally fault others for letting social niceties make them such willing prey.

Except that I shouldn't exult in a short-lived win for me and possibly even a net loss. And that smile wasn't self-deprecation so much as barely concealed shame.

Social and cultural courtesies can exist for many reasons beyond their obviously being the right thing to do.

Maybe the reason is basic respect, such as when we stand up when someone older approaches the table to sit down with us.

Maybe it's expediency, like when we let someone else take the next oncoming taxi because they look to be in a hurry.

Maybe it's recognition that they already have it harder, like when we install a button next to the door so it can be opened by someone in a wheelchair with a lot less effort.

But one thing is clear: we engage in and offer those courtesies in a way that conveys the intent behind them. The respect we want to convey is obvious when we stand up; the slight nod or wave from someone who took the taxi we passed on is equally plain in its graciousness. And for someone who needs accessible options, offering them also means conveying that we are, and must always be, inclusive.

In an inclusive society, something that starts off as a courtesy can eventually be codified. For good reason too. Not everyone will be aware of the worth and validity of those courtesies. But, if a sizeable group does accept them, this hopefully ensures they never disappear from civilized society. It's what I've always understood as the reason behind laws—offering a handout may be generosity, but offering a leg up is sometimes a necessity.

However, there's another side to that coin when common courtesies begin to be perceived as entitlements. At that point, omission of courtesy translates in our heads as injury. And there's nothing quite so self-righteous as perceived injury.

For every instance I've been with someone who's punched the elevator button for me, someone else has failed to hold the door open. And after much wasted energy, I realized that I would probably be happier in this world if I acknowledged the kindness of the first act and disregarded the thoughtlessness of the second.

In my workday, I walk past many of those access buttons and think about the simple elegance of that solution. It provides accessible options to those who need them but is a reminder that they will still have to go through the door themselves.

Those buttons also remind me that, yes, I've had help and a lot of it. Some of it was given magnanimously, and some of it was explicitly asked for. But all of it was given without precondition, without assumption, and without judgment; it expected nothing less and nothing more from me than it did from anyone else.

And you know what that means? The next time you're headed towards a door where I'm standing and your arms are over-loaded with stuff, just let me hold it open for you.

It's really the least I could do.

FEAR

Next time you're standing up, plant your left foot down all the way from the hip like it's one solid block of stone.

Now, with that left leg and rotated hip still glued to the spot, lift your right leg to begin your stride.

Finally, complete your stride and rotate your left leg from the hip to a point where you feel balanced and comfortable.

Repeat these steps as needed to move forward.

Congratulations, you've now learned my basic rules of walking.

Wait, no; there are a few more: you need to rotate that hip into your stride, not drag it. Make sure you distribute your weight evenly between both legs, or else your shoulders will ache. And you need to keep your paces short and evenly sized so that you don't tire yourself out.

That should be it, really.

But just as a matter of endurance, you also shouldn't hop because it will strain your arms. Imagine two elbow crutches at your sides. When the surface is slippery, plant the crutches straight down so that they don't slide.

While you're at it, avoid mud, avoid sand, avoid the pointier pebbles on a dirt road; avoid the big stones, the little stones, wet surfaces, marble, and granite. Best to avoid carpets as well since they can curl up and trip you. Stay away from crowded streets to avoid getting shoved, and never be alone on empty streets without help ...

Chances are, for however long you've walked, your brain has instinctively known the rules and when your brain instructs your legs, they cooperate.

For each of my steps, I think through where my feet need to go, where they might slip, where they would be improperly placed, and finally, where they should go. The difference between you and me is that I do this deliberately, every time, and sometimes my brain and my legs don't feel like they agree. The odds of your acquired instincts failing are far, far slimmer than mine are as I solve physics by committee.

Since I first learned this manner of walking, I've gone through those calculations in my head many, many times. Written out, the instructions might seem overwhelming, but like anything with years of practice, an explanation is actually way harder than the execution.

I don't know, for example, why I always lead with my right leg before my left leg; maybe it's my version of riding a bike or learning to play the piano. Following these calculations to their end before every step feels right; it makes sense, but above all, it feels safe.

Maybe that's really what they're for: ensuring that I don't fall. Or more precisely, that I am able to get back up again. They're the reason I've never been afraid of falling and why I've assumed that every fall simply involved a calculation I hadn't yet added to my repertoire. My rules for walking are the assurance I need that I've figured out where I am, what I need to do to get around, and, perhaps most pressingly, where that next step goes. Those rules are proof that I've understood the system within which I operate.

I'd been in school for twelve years and university for two before I realized that systems could dramatically change. I'd traveled for my internship, and Paris wasn't Delhi, and my youth hostel wasn't our house. I'd assumed for fourteen years that Ma or Appa would know how to get me to school and I wouldn't need to; now, I stood in a French suburb wondering if I could actually board a bus myself and commute. I still wasn't scared of falling on the bus or off it, and while I started to feel the pangs of uncertainty that come with being in an unfamiliar place and without familiar people, I still retained one key life skill.

For years, I'd learned everything by watching those around me and I am nothing if not a consummate imitator. For the rest of my stay in Paris, I did everything exactly as my other intern friends did and entrusted all my decisions to them. They stabilized in their system quicker than I did, and by watching their next step I learned to calculate mine.

A year later, when I moved to Providence to study, I knew what I needed to do and I knew that I'd figure out the rules once more. However, this time I missed something and it haunted me.

During my first semester there I became unwell for a week. As I curled up on my bed frantically trying to engineer my next move, I heard the clatter of steps outside my dorm room and a knock on my door. Before I had a chance to lift my pain-wracked body from the bed, a muffled voice came from a few rooms down, and the steps disappeared to the far side of the corridor.

Eventually, I ended up getting myself to the clinic and it took a hospital stay and multiple courses of medication to get me back to my fellow grad students in the computer science building. But, as they regaled me stories about what I'd missed, I could still hear that muffled voice saying, "Yeah, he doesn't really like to join in much, maybe just go to the next door down."

Imitation works for stabilizing systems and avoiding falls, but there's no substitute for actually knowing people to assist with getting back up when unexpected falls happen.

A year after that, I moved to Redmond. It was the third unfamiliar place in as many years. But this time, I considered myself better prepared for what a move entailed. It mattered little that I knew very few people, and it mattered even less that my health hadn't really improved. I would stabilize this system by learning from others, and I would learn to rely on them and trust them to stabilize me during headwinds. I was ready with my training, my improvisation, my plan, and even my backup plan for when that first plan failed. Personnel shifts happened frequently as did how and where I worked, but through it all, I was lucky to have a common group of friends and coworkers who looked out for me.

I had wanted a fair shot at life, I now had one, and I'd still never once been scared.

Just months prior to my thirtieth birthday, work had drastically changed, as had my responsibilities. It wasn't a big deal because I had experience on my side, and from my previous travels, I'd learned how to figure out new systems. Even though things were moving fast, this is where my plans would come in handy if only I could apply them as quickly as possible.

And yet, in all the chaos, I forgot that moving fast for me came with a cost; although I'd learned to accommodate any regressions in my health, all I could really claim was delayed failure, not success.

For weeks, I found myself in an intense loop of professional success, followed by a period of physical relapse, agony, and recovery. And during one of those loops with my body laid out on a couch, my fingers clenched and back arched in pain, fear finally wormed in: maybe, I thought, today's the day I'd stop being useful.

Let me confess something here: when it comes to my disability, I am a pragmatist. I do not ascribe to the rose-tinted glasses version of life that has me walking well into my nineties. Equally, I do not assume that the mere existence of my disability negates all opportunities for me. Given a chance, I know I can do just as well as anybody else. But I do not doubt that others will be able to continue far longer than I will. There's an end date on my utility, and I'm aware that it'll arrive sooner for me than it will for other people.

Yet in all my years of education, travel, and work, that date seemed far off, and I started believing it might never arrive.

The truly insidious thing about that fear is how it twists that very success against you. Yes, I'd completed my education, but what if workplaces weren't controlled environments like school? Yes, I'd had a career for over a decade, but what if I was moved to a team with responsibilities I couldn't meet? Yes, I was in a role where I could deliver what I was asked, but what if that ended tomorrow?

More than most people, I'm acutely aware that the point I am at today is a carefully orchestrated sequence of events. But what if tomorrow it grinds to a halt?

What if, my fearful brain asked, there came a day when every single one of my rules, plans, and calculations failed?

For nearly three decades, whenever I wanted something badly enough, I'd push till I got it. I had rebelled against anyone telling me not to be ambitious, competitive, or independent. I'd work the hours, or I'd work the system, and I'd get what I wanted. But how does one even begin to fight the doubts of their own fearful brain when those doubts made me want to hide away from everyone else?

In six months, I went from, "I want to do something, but I don't know how yet" to, "I could do something, but I don't want to."

For six months, a far worse agony slowly took over my mind. I recalled my childhood and Ma's tear-stained expression of helplessness when I was unwell and screaming. I remembered Appa's panic-filled face when he couldn't figure out why I couldn't find relief. I remembered Dee's furrowed brow as she tried to apply her entire medical training to understand what was hurting me.

For six months, when my body braced for the pain, I could only think of all that effort put into me throughout my life. And I no longer felt deserving of that effort.

And then something very simple happened.

I'd been moving aimlessly about at work, and a friend of mine asked me for my opinion on something he was working on. He didn't seem satisfied with my listless recitation of facts and asked me to pick up that task instead. I turned it around in my head and dismissed it as an unnecessary software trinket. Walking back to my desk after our chat, another friend asked me over lunch to catch him up on what I was doing and I mentioned this task in passing. He excitedly pointed out how challenging that task was and how complex that system would be, and something clicked.

If you've experienced that kind of pain, I don't know how you erased it. I don't think I have or ever will, but I know I stopped thinking about it as often after that day.

That fear is still in there in my head, it never goes away, but I can look away from it every time I have something else to do.

Fear

Lunches help when you can talk to a friend.

Dinners on Fridays help, where silly things make you laugh.

A mentor's suggestion to take swimming lessons helps where, for an hour, that fear is forgotten.

And as the fear gets pushed farther and farther back, other parts of me come slowly back to life.

People describe the life of a disabled person in a variety of ways, but I've long believed that it closely resembles a scientific experiment. We're aware of its constructs, and we're aware of its parameters, but we're never certain of its outcomes. Every successful trial increases our confidence in the foundational hypotheses of the experiment, and every failed trial informs us of a gap.

And even though my life's experiment has survived for as long as it has, I can only claim a delay of failure rather than conclusive success. A long series of successes may be overshadowed by a single failure, but the cloud of that single failure might dissipate with the briefest sunburst of success.

My simple reality is that all the rules and all the calculations cannot forestall my eventual fate.

One day, I'll stop being useful, but I won't allow tomorrow to be that day.

SAFE

I suppose every family has their traditions. And as a child, you adopt them not because you understand them but because you do as you're told.

Once I moved to Redmond, it fell upon me to start my own traditions, and I decided on one pretty quickly: every December, I'd try to fly back to Delhi to celebrate my birthday. It's the rare tradition that marries timing (work tapers down towards the end of the year) with convenience (I get to ring in the new year with family).

Every year, on my birthday, we go to the same temple, our temple, for about an hour, and Ma and Appa make an offering in my name. Every year, I ask them, "Shouldn't I know how to do this myself?" and every year Appa tells me, "Maybe next year." (That's the other tradition of these trips in December: I somehow leave Redmond in my thirties and land in Delhi a ten-year-old.)

The temple is about a fifteen-minute drive away from our house, and once you survive the traffic, the parking, and the weirdly high step up to the sidewalk, you enter its outer perimeter. This is where you're expected to take off your shoes before you enter the actual temple premises.

When I was younger, one of the temple staff would rush up with a chair for me to sit on while Ma took off my shoes. These days he still tries, but Ma waves him away; it's harder for her to bend down, and it's easier to reach my shoes if I lift my feet instead. Every time she does this, I'm reminded of the fact that touching someone's feet is a sign of affectionate respect, and I should be touching hers; that after taking so much from so many, I've never bent down myself.

When she's done removing both shoes, she gives me a wide grin and says, "Ready?" before she walks over to wash her hands; you don't approach the inner sanctum with mud caked on your fingers. Meanwhile, as I'm getting up, Appa—ever the overachiever—is already done washing his hands and feet.

I gingerly walk over to the massive temple door and lift myself over the threshold leading onto its marble floor. I've come here since I was five, and I continue to be surprised at how the noise outside the walls simply dissolves away. Appa has already made his way in and is chit-chatting with the priests.

I try to keep up, but the marble floor has always been a challenge. I tell myself that I just need to be careful and concentrate on where I'm planting my crutches.

"Don't look down, look up," a voice behind me commands; Ma's just a few steps behind me and has seen me commit the cardinal sin when it comes to walking with prosthetics. I had been so absorbed in placing my feet correctly that I kept staring down at the floor, at the rugs spread out to supply some small relief to those who come for morning prayers in the Delhi winter. It turns out that when you're worrying about slipping or tripping, you miss the massive pillar looming about five paces in front of you.

I look up and notice that one of the avatars of Vishnu sculpted into said pillar is smiling at me. Having noticed my confusion, is that a smile of contentment or contempt on his face? Seems as good a place as any to pause for a break and find out; I also finally exhale the breath I realize I've been holding since I passed through the temple doors.

"Just relax, and don't put so much pressure on your shoulders; now remember, lead with the right, make sure you're steady, then bear down and lift the left …"

It's the voice of my very first prosthetist, who has taken it upon himself to help me walk again. There's a group of other doctors standing by, hoping I'll follow his instructions more closely this time. I desperately want to because of all the anxious faces watching me, but my brain refuses to accept that walking is something it ever knew to perform. I plant my right foot down, and it locks in place; step one is done. I tilt slightly to the right side and transfer my weight as quickly as I can; step two is nearly there. Suddenly, it occurs to me that I'm not sure whether my right leg will remain locked, and my head tilts to check. Four voices at once murmur, "Look up!" and when my head snaps up at once in response, my mind's forgotten about step three. I suspect that "Don't fall on your shoulder" wasn't their intent when talking about pressure, but more irritatingly, I think looking down could've avoided the whole fall.

"Why do I have to look up? I don't know if the leg is at the right place, I have to check!"

"It'll be fine, it won't lock in any other position, and you'll know …"

"But I'll fall if I don't check!"

"No, you won't—we're all here, and if you start to fall, we'll catch you … see that uncle over there? That's why he's standing so close to you …"

"Okay … so I should look at you when I lift the left leg?"

"Yes, if you want to look down sometimes, that's okay, but you have to practice the other way too … ready? Good, let's try again, from here to the wall."

"Shrivaths, come over here …"

Appa's call snaps me out of the arguments of my five-year-old self; he's calling my name and gesturing me to come closer to the sanctum. Time to walk over the rugs now, which should be easy, just need to be careful over the creases.

A few minutes later, I'm at the base of the steps leading up to the idols, and the priests beginning their prayers briefly pause to look back at me. I gawk at the marble steps, and one of them realizes I might need help making my way up. He starts in my direction, but I decide I'm safer at the base and wave him off. Ma helpfully jumps in with, "Don't worry, you can pray from down there; it's okay," and I nod in relieved agreement.

I used to insist on making my way up those steps when I was younger, but I don't any longer, not unless my family insists, in fact. And they're less eager to insist these days too. I try to lean back a little, which reminds me that this version of my prosthetics doesn't include heels; standing on the balls of my feet just means more strain on the arms and the shoulders, but maybe the prayers won't be very long.

"Did you see it?"

Part 4

It's the voice of my prosthetist again, talking to the teenage version of me.

There isn't much space to walk, but somehow, we've got a stretch without any furniture or people crowding it. This new pair of limbs I'm test-driving is supposed to get me through university, but apparently, I'm not using them properly. It's been more than a decade since I started wearing prosthetics and I highly doubt user error can be a factor anymore, but my prosthetist disagrees. And to prove his point, he directs me to a full-length mirror nearby, just to pinpoint the problem. He's hoping I'll notice the flaw in this perfectly crafted experiment.

"You missed it, didn't you? Your left leg is hopping with no weight on it."

"No, I put my weight on it just like you said."

"You're not looking at the mirror, look ahead when you walk, and you'll see what I mean."

"I can't always look in the mirror; I have to see where I place the crutch."

"You know where to place the crutch already. You've been doing this long enough," Appa chimes in, "Do as he says."

The only thing worse than one's experience being overruled is being both experienced and wrong at the same time. My left arm does ache more often these days than the right, and sure enough, I can now see it in the mirror too. Looks like my walking algorithm is showing its age, too; I'm trying to move faster, but it looks like I'm just moving more painfully. I'm sixteen; is it only going to get faster from now on? God, now the right arm is hurting too ...

"Are you sure you don't want me to get you a chair?"

I'm back in the temple again, and the same staff member from earlier is looking at me with concern. Maybe because my arms are shaking slightly, trying to keep the same rigid posture as the idols in front of me. I wave him off again, and he wanders off unconvinced.

Eventually, Ma walks down and nods at me; the prayers are complete. Appa is still deep in conversation with the priests, but she and I start walking away. Nearly done, just need to put on my shoes, and I can be on stable footing again. One of the priests calls out for Ma from behind us, and she asks me to keep walking to the benches; she'll meet me there after she's picked up the rest of the prasadam, the prayer offering.

The evening crowd is starting to filter in and find their spots on the prayer rugs. I decide that it would be rude of me to rush past them on my way out, so I walk back to the pillar and lean against it. That sculpture is smiling at me again. Why did its expression seem so contemptuous before? What does it see that I don't?

"It's the dumbest thing, I don't know why my prosthetist keeps nagging me about looking ahead the whole time ..."

"I don't know, it makes some sense." It's my friend now, responding to the complaints of teenage me as we walk to the family car parked at our school gate. "If you were crossing the street, you'd look in front," he suggests.

My friend is tagging along because I can't be trusted on rainy days (his words, not mine) and the last time that I walked by myself to the parking lot, I'd slipped on something.

"Whatever," I argue again. "What if it's like today? What if there are wet leaves on the street? Shouldn't I be looking down to avoid them?"

"How often are there going to be wet leaves on city streets?"

"I don't know! What if I have to live in a place where it rains all the time?"

"Yeah, sure, why not? And you're surrounded by trees," he says, rolling his eyes, "Won't you still see the wet leaves first if you're looking ahead? I don't think your doctor means to stare at the sky."

"It just seems so pointless; our teachers aren't looking up when they're walking around during exams. And that guy in our class, the smart one, he's always walking with his head down, deep in thought."

"Maybe, but he also doesn't have to worry about falling on wet leaves. He can stand up again on his own; he's pretty intelligent that way. Maybe he's so intelligent that he can look down and ahead at the same time."

"I'm 'pretty intelligent' too, you know," I retort to my friend. "Why do you think you're here with me?"

"Ready to go?" Ma interrupts as she gestures to the bench. I slowly make my way as she follows a step behind, two pairs of shoes in hand. Putting the shoes on is slightly harder; it requires more effort for the shoe to snap in place. It's another one of those things we've learned over time, and Ma and I have a rhythm to it now.

"Done," she announces, again with that grin and a slap on my kneecaps. Appa is standing near the outer doors to walk back to the car with us.

Another wash of the hands, another slight bow to the gods within the sanctum, and another annual visit to the temple is behind us. My parents are again granted a modicum of peace that wherever I go, whatever I do, those watchful eyes from within the temple will keep me safe.

That visit every year, where I feel the most unsafe standing on tiptoe, where I worry about the slippery marble floor, where my mind and body are at their most rigid and tensed, is the one that cloaks me in my family's faith each year.

And each year, as I stare at the idols in the sanctum, the paintings on the walls, and the sculptures in each pillar, I'm reminded that faith doesn't always follow a single direction. It is my instinct towards safety and self-preservation that compels me to look down, to concentrate on what is under my feet as I walk. But it's also an admission of doubt that those around me will protect me when I fall.

For most of my life, chance or intent forced me down certain paths where I'd been looking down, up, and ahead without knowing it; if I'd kept looking down after university, for instance, I'd never have made it to Paris, Providence, or Redmond.

Truly, it's why my years of poor health hurt so much more—I think best when I can trust myself, I trust myself the most when I can look ahead, and I look ahead most often when I walk. When I don't—or can't—walk, I look down, and I'm completely seized by the need for survival above all else.

Looking ahead carries a kind of reckless self-assurance, but it also safeguards me from insisting on certainty for every step I take. It is an exercise not just in anticipation but also of confidence, of understanding the immediate well enough that the future can matter.

Safe

Since I came to Redmond, I've been through multiple falls that broke my body and a period of illness that broke my mind. And yet, I know I need to get up and walk onward because that's how I know I can feel safe. It's how I reciprocate the trust of those who've protected me all my life. It's how I can go to our temple year after year and look that sculpture in the eye.

Despite my best attempts, there are years that strain any attempt to keep tradition. Such times are painful because I know I was made for so much more than survival alone.

One such year, I sat alone in my house in Redmond on my birthday. I thought about family and friends instead of wet leaves on city streets. Life had slowed down and sped up at the same time, so I had to force myself to look up and ahead.

I finally understood why that sculpture was smiling at me. I had always hoped it was a smile of contentment and worried it was a smirk of contempt. But now I believe it has always been a smile of faith in someone who chooses to walk again after every fall.

EQUAL

Every so often, when I close my eyes, I'm back home, at our house in Delhi, and I'm standing in front of the bookcase in our living room. Over the years that bookcase has morphed into an entertainment unit, a storage space for musical instruments, and the focal point of religious ceremonies performed at our house. What I always remember about it is just how tall it felt, particularly when I was on the floor. I could look up, and its shelves seemed to go on forever, stretching as high up as my eyes could go. (It's the same shelf where all the grown-up books were always placed tantalizingly out of my reach.)

One of the books I could reach, when I was only seven, was a trivia book stuffed with all kinds of miscellany. As I flipped through it, I unexpectedly came across a section focused on facts about famous people with disabilities.

Reading this book was the first time I realized that the Braille script was named after someone, that Helen Keller lived a full life without sight or speech, and that Beethoven was composing some of his greatest music after his hearing began to weaken.

It seems odd to say this, but till then, I didn't know of anyone notable who was even remotely like me. Sure, I went with my parents to clinics and prosthetists and rehab centers, but everyone I saw there seemed on par with where I was. The patients I saw, the kids I met, even their parents, everyone seemed to be trying to figure life out, and I wanted so much more than just that.

Meanwhile, the famous people in these stories seemingly had it sorted. Put simply and crassly, until I'd read those stories, I didn't know of anyone like me who'd won.

And then I read about someone who'd won and then some: a British RAF fighter pilot named Douglas Bader.

Group Captain Douglas Bader trained as a pilot in the UK at the age of eighteen. Then, while performing some aerobatic maneuvers at an airshow in 1931, his plane crashed and he lost his legs. He was retired from the RAF against his will. His written summary of the events that led to his disability simply read: "crashed slow-rolling near ground. bad show."

After he survived recovery, he retrained as a pilot, passed his flight checks, and requested reactivation. But he was repeatedly knocked back.

Then the Second World War broke out and Bader was finally allowed to rejoin the RAF due to a critical shortage of pilots. He scored multiple air victories in his second run as a flying ace and commanded a squadron that rewarded his perseverance by growing into an efficient fighting unit. He campaigned for more aggressive tactics and even survived being captured and held as a prisoner of war.

Douglas Bader continued to work after his second retirement from the RAF a year later. Although—according to some accounts—he was headstrong, blunt, even arrogant, his life passed into legend.

It's one hell of a story.

Now, yes, I'll concede that there are several obvious reasons why the story of a dashing air force pilot with no legs would draw the attention of a seven-year-old boy with a vivid imagination and no legs. And yes, it's the sort of pull-yourself-up-by-your-bootstraps story that most people would want to share with that boy to prove that, with grit and determination, he too could achieve great things.

But then those stories faded in my memory for many years. They found me again nearly three decades later and I started thinking more deeply about their early hold on me. I saw them in a way that my seven-year-old self never did.

Curiously enough, as I thought about Douglas Bader, the answers to "How did I make it this far?" started to become clearer.

There are a few different ways to look at people who have a disability. The most automatic is perhaps merely noting an absence or lack of something that others take for granted. This reductive thinking, however, fails to make space for the reality that absence and lack are where creativity and invention live.

Absence or lack is where the optimism of engineering and technology can meet the gaps of present reality for some and build an improved reality for everyone.

Most humans never needed a computer, but our lives are now immeasurably easier with one.

Most of us don't need a tactile script to touch-read text, but our lives are better with the companionship and contributions of those who can read books written in Braille.

The same could be said for moving walkways, elevators, ramps, motorized vehicles, reading glasses—many of which were invented due to a felt absence or lack.

That outsized attention on what's "missing" obscures our awareness of everything else.

Keller couldn't see, hear, or speak, but she wanted to study and communicate, just like everyone else. Braille wanted to read his books after he lost his sight, and Beethoven wanted to continue making music even though his ears were failing him.

Knowing what we now know of their lives, would we want to deny them their ambitions because it would be too hard or deprive them of rivalries because of perceived "fairness" issues?

Think about it. Would you have been one of the people refusing Douglas Bader when he said he wanted to fly again?

Douglas Bader actually claimed to be a better pilot with his "tin legs." Most pilots would black out during tight turns because the G forces would force their blood down to their lower limbs; Bader had no lower limbs, so he could stay conscious for longer.

Then, when his plane went down in enemy territory, one of those tin legs was torn off and he reflected that if he'd still had legs made of flesh he would have bled out on the ground. By a fortunate turn of events, a British plane was even allowed to parachute in a new set of legs for him while he was a prisoner of war. He tried to escape so often on those legs that his captors began to describe this man with no legs as someone who "walks well with stick." (When they'd had enough of his escapades, they sent him off to an "escape-proof" camp from which he was liberated when the war ended.)

The point of all these true-life stories is that when people are obsessing about perceived absence and lack in others, they often miss the creativity, inventiveness, and personality of the person standing right in front of them.

In other words, they miss truly seeing someone like me.

The stories of Bader and Beethoven, Keller and Hawking, Braille and Zanardi and others, aren't user manuals or self-congratulatory tales. They're descriptions of the slow, grinding, plodding day-to-day involved in living with a disability. They're calls to action, to allow more creative and inventive players into the game.

These stories are also reminders that seeing someone live up to their potential first requires expecting more of them. Inertia has a powerful grip, but if you expect more of me—rather than presuming inadequacy—I promise I'll do whatever's necessary to prove you right.

You know how I know all this to be true? Because it's what everyone around me has been doing for me for as long as I've known them. Their plan—my plan—has worked because the people in my life understood the implications of those stories even before I realized them myself. They've constantly expected creativity, inventiveness, and grit, so I delivered. Most importantly, they've kept me grounded and connected when I was tempted to give up. It's why I prefer to focus on my people and what they taught me rather than the events of that day in '88. Their refusal to focus on absence and lack is the reason I can have this conversation with you today. The ambition of their plan mattered far more than its substance—when it demanded better, it compelled me to be better, for myself and for everyone who made me.

There are many more people I wish I could tell you about:

My primary school teacher who tutored me at home to get me into Class 1.

Our driver who drove me to school and to university, to parties and to exams.

The families who helped me in Chicago, in Boston, in Providence, in Paris, in every Indian city I visited.

But this is a conversation where I've talked for far too long, so I should really wrap up.

Enough has changed since that thirtieth birthday that I'll need new legs again soon. These legs will come with their usual reminders: walk, don't hop; look up and ahead. There'll be another few months while I get used to walking with them, but whatever I've learned over the years will come back to me, just like these stories have.

And this time, I'll remind myself of one more thing: walking with crutches isn't supposed to look normal because it's not, and it never will be. It's no longer what I even want.

I don't want to be normal anymore.

I want to be your equal.

Not some exalted more-than and certainly not some inadequate less-than.

My plan isn't to walk the way you do, but to be allowed to fall in ways you can.

And when you treat me as your equal I'd love to walk with you, forget about my voice and listen to yours.

Trust me when I tell you that you always tell one hell of a story.

AFTERWORD

When I first started sketching these essays, I only knew the ideas I wanted to write about and couldn't quite see what connected them. I didn't want it to be about my accident because I remembered so little of it. While it is about the events of my life and my disability, I wanted this book to be about something more. So, when I thought about these questions, I knew what to write but it wasn't till I re-read my answers that themes emerged and stitched my notes together for me. There's just one final note on why I cared so much about needing a plan.

My identity can be expressed as the conjunction of a fleshy half and a metallic half because my whole life since '88 has been engineered.

What you see, what you talk to, is the fleshy half, and it might be comforting to assume that's all there is. That half still prefers to watch every step but ignore the risk, believing that when I fall I can simply get up and walk again.

But if you wonder how I've gotten this far, you should look carefully at the rest of me. You'll see that true creativity lies not in that fleshy half but in the carefully engineered components that empower the rest of me to move and grow.

Three decades ago, when I began, all I had was a single requirement: survival. But those who remade me saw far beyond basic survival and carefully designed the architecture that would give me the best chance at truly living.

The rest, whatever I've accomplished since, is simply implementation.

THANKS

I can't believe that we're both now at the end of this book. Thank you for patiently reading it all the way through and I hope you'll indulge me with a few more paragraphs to share how this book came to be. Much like the story in these pages, the eight years of writing this book also went through phases of ambition, confusion, and clarity. That you can finally hold it in your hands is entirely due to the nudging and pushing from those around me who believed that you'd want to know this story.

The ideas in this book first came about at my lowest ebb when Brian Lapinski and Kamran Saeed thought that a dinner with friends might cheer me up. Since then, that Thursday/Sunday dinner or lunch with Brian, Kamran, and Lavinder Singh has been where noise filters out of my life and leaves me feeling lighter. Thanks also to Jerry de Raad, Mark Flick, and Nick Horvath, who taught me to once again face my fear head on instead of warily looking at it from a distance. I consider myself privileged to have had friends and mentors who thought more highly of me than I often did myself.

When I first met Carrie Olesen, I thought she'd be another one of those people who I meet at the top of a stairwell and with whom the conversation ends when the stairs do. I'm glad I was so absurdly wrong because Carrie read every one of the early drafts of my chapters and her feedback infused her considerable empathy into my writing. Thank you, Carrie, and I hope this version has fewer commas than the ones you read.

Thank you to Soundarya Balasubramani, Rajesh Setty, Raji Rajagopalan, Dona Sarkar, Bethany Kelly, and Anaik Alcasas for seeing this book through to the finish line. If I hadn't met you, I'd still probably be writing that one more chapter or making that one last tweak that I felt the book still needed. You believed that this story was worth telling and turned my text into this book.

I'm thankful to Nazar Abdelrahman for many, many things but this book benefited most from two things he taught me: be clear and be prepared. I know no one else who's as relentless about presenting the clearest argument and foreseeing every last move on the chessboard. And yet, the themes I wanted to talk about in this book were complex enough that I could only find comfort with applying his precepts. For that training, and for his friendship, I'll always remain in Nazar's debt.

To my friends at grad school, university, and various primary and secondary schools: I hope I did our rivalry justice and I lived up to the game. To the teachers who've graciously persisted in giving me an education despite my illness, idiosyncrasy, and indiscretions: thank you for the encouragement you gave me when the alternative could've been so much easier. To the medical staff who got me walking again, and the disability activists who've made the road easy for me to walk on: thank you for what you've made possible.

I'm still not quite sure what alchemy of events drew Maddie into my life, but I was certain that she'd soon walk away from this chatty, wordy, unruly human sitting across from her. As I repeatedly emphasized to her that she could do so much better than our conversation, I found myself desperately wanting to explain myself to her too. So, Maddie patiently read the book and has patiently tried to understand me. She listened through all the calculations I'd make before a walk and then pointed out that I still hadn't taken the first step. She trudged out on a wintry night to send a picture of the stairs in front of her house so I could assure both of us that we could meet there. For every "Why" I've had, Maddie has challenged me with a "Why not" and I hope to live up to her affection and her ambitions for me.

Thanks

A final word then about the main characters of my story: my family. I read once about a moment that most inventors experience in their lives that changes them forever. It's a moment of realization that the stuff they use every day wasn't born; it was made. An artist, an inventor, an engineer, somebody made that world-changing thing in their lives. Even more importantly, that they're "somebody" too and they too could change the world around them. As I wrote this book, I experienced that same clarity myself and realized how inventive my family has been. When they saw the elements of a full life—education, employment, family—they saw it as inventors do. They realized early on that they were "somebody" and that life wasn't given, it was made. This book is their story as much as it is mine. So Ma, Appa, Dee, Jeej, and my wonderful niece: I get it now. I know that I'm "somebody" and I'll continue to make something in my life too.

R Shrivaths Iyengar

Thanks

AUTHOR BIO

S hrivaths Iyengar was born in New Delhi, India and carries that city's improvisational spirit within him to this day. He attended the Indian Institute of Technology, Delhi, as an undergraduate, and Brown University for his Masters. He has worked at Microsoft as a software engineer for close to two decades. *Hitting My Stride: An Engineer's Notes on Disability* is his first book and describes how his family and their mindset has shaped his perspectives towards his disability.

www.ingramcontent.com/pod-product-compliance
Lightning Source LLC
Chambersburg PA
CBHW060527150626
46553CB00023B/605